THE PREPPER'S CANNING GUIDE

THE PREPPER'S CANNING GUIDE

Affordably Stockpile a Lifesaving Supply of Nutritious, Delicious, Shelf-Stable Foods

DAISY LUTHER

ULYSSES PRESS

Published in the United States by:
Ulysses Press
P.O. Box 3440
Berkeley, CA 94703
www.ulyssespress.com

ISBN: 978-1-61243-664-7
Library of Congress Control Number: 2016957543

Printed in Canada by Marquis Book Printing
10 9 8 7 6 5 4

Acquisitions editor: Casie Vogel
Managing editor: Claire Chun
Editor: Shayna Keyles
Proofreader: Lauren Harrison
Index: Sayre Van Young
Front cover design: what!design @ whatweb.com
Interior design: Jake Flaherty
Cover artwork: © Tim Masters/shutterstock.com;
    jar icon © Oleh Markov/shutterstock.com

*This book is dedicated to two wonderful Southern cooks:
my dear friend Bernadine, who is over 100 years old and still
cooking from scratch every day, and in memory of my Granny,
who was a wonderful cook and the sweetest lady I've ever known.*

Contents

Introduction

From time immemorial, preserving the harvest has been a vital step in preparing for the barren winter months ahead. Indeed, the agrarian lifestyle was based on producing food and then preserving enough of it to last until your next harvest. Now we can combine agrarian tradition with science and modern food safety. The tools and knowledge available today allow us to preserve our harvests in ways our ancestors never dreamed of.

Different methods of preservation have been used throughout the ages and many of them are still used today, but hands down, my favorite method of preservation is canning. Canning is the perfect solution for those seeking natural food sources, for gardeners, for those seeking a more self-reliant life, and for those interested in preparedness.

A prepper's pantry is usually loaded to the rafters with things like beans, rice, and wheat, but many food stockpiles are lacking when it comes to storing proteins, fruits, and vegetables. Home canning fills in the gaps in a pantry stocked with store-bought goods, and does so at a very reasonable price. For home canners, a hot meal during a power outage situation can be as simple as opening a jar, pouring the contents into a pot, and placing it on the wood stove for about half an hour.

Once you have a pressure canner (and you conquer the fear of blowing yourself up with it!), you can preserve nearly anything. By creating meals right in jars, you can provide your family with instant, tasty nutrition. These items are very simple to prepare. If you use garden produce when possible and use ingredients purchased on sale, you can have many "instant" meals prepared at a very affordable price—and the best part is, you know exactly what's in each of them.

In this book, we'll go through canning step by step. First we'll discuss why canning is a great way for preppers to preserve their food, we'll discuss safety, and we'll talk about the basics of canning. Even if you've never canned before, you'll have all of the information you need to get started.

Next you'll find the recipes. If you've never canned before, water bath canning jams and condiments is a great way to get started. Once you've gotten your feet wet with these recipes, you can move on to pressure canning individual ingredients. Then, for the crowning jewel of canning projects, we'll can some entire meals that are ready to heat and eat. You'll turn to those meals again and again over the course of the year—trust me; they're so good that you won't want to wait for a power outage! If you're a veteran canner, you'll find new charts to refer to, new recipes to try, and new guidelines for safely canning your own recipes. I hope that this book becomes a reference you will turn to again and again.

I wrote a canning book called *The Organic Canner* several years ago, and the biggest difference you'll find is that this book was written *by* a prepper, *for* preppers. There are an additional 15,000 words in this book, and much of the new information is related to preparedness. You will find some tried and true recipes, some modified versions of old recipes, and some brand-spanking new ones that my family has enjoyed since the first book came out. Because food scientists are constantly learning and updating their findings, all recipes in this book have been updated to reflect the newest information and some recipes from the previous book have been omitted because they've been found to be unsafe.

So dust off your canner, and let's use some modern technology to get prepared the old-fashioned way.

PART 1

Canning Basics for the Prepper

CHAPTER 1

A Prepper's Guide to Canning

Most preppers have cupboards, attics, and spare rooms full of beans, rice, and other grains. Some stash grocery-store bargain finds made of cheap, non-nutritious ingredients. Still others fill their deep freezers with meat, fruits, and vegetables and plan to rely on a generator and a fuel supply to keep their food safe to eat.

However, there are several problems with pantries that hold only these types of supplies.

- Beans, rice, and whole grains take a long time to cook, and a long time equals a lot of fuel. In the summer, you won't want a blazing fire heating up your house for that long, and in the winter, you may go through too much valuable fuel.

- Eating the same thing again and again is boring and can lead to food fatigue. Food fatigue occurs when a person gets so tired of eating the same thing that they'd rather not eat at all. During a crisis, you need the energy that comes from plenty of nutrition, so it's best to avoid food fatigue.

- A limited pantry means limited variety in nutrients, and this can lead to malnutrition and other illnesses.

- Shelf-stable meat can be very expensive to purchase, and the price for a high-quality product can be completely out of reach for many families.

- Relying on the power grid to keep your meat, fruits, and vegetables preserved is risky. Even with a generator, eventually you'll run out of fuel, and then all of that food will go to waste unless you quickly preserve it through other means.

While all of the items mentioned above may have a place in your pantry, there's another way to build your food supply on an annual basis: home canning. Canning is an old-fashioned art that when combined with modern food safety science can create a safe, healthy, and delicious food supply for your family.

When you preserve your own food, you know exactly what is in the jars on your shelves. You can avoid allergens, genetically modified ingredients, and excess salt or sugar. What's more, you won't be reliant on a grid that could fail at any time, either for storing your food or for consuming it— when you can your own meals in jars, your food is always fully cooked. Although it will be more appetizing heated up, you can safely consume canned food straight from the jar.

If a grid-down situation goes on for an extended time, it will be important to have a long-term, grid-independent method for preserving your harvest and your meat. In my family, we already practice the concept of an agrarian pantry, which I wrote about in my book *The Pantry Primer: A Prepper's Guide to Whole Food on a Half Price Budget*. An agrarian pantry is similar to what our ancestors had. Most purchases are made during the growing season and only small shopping trips are needed to supplement these throughout the year. To build an agrarian pantry, stock up on a year's supply of basics like grains, baking items, tea, coffee, and dried beans. Then focus your efforts on acquiring items when they are in season and preserving them when they are at their peak. Try your hand at canning, dehydrating, and root cellaring. Items can be grown on your own property or purchased by the bushel from local farms and orchards.

Look into purchasing a side of beef and a side of pork to add to your pantry. One purchase per year is sufficient for most families and the price per pound drops dramatically when you buy meat in these large quantities. Remember not to put all of your faith in the deep freezer, however, because a grid-down scenario could leave you with a smelly mess and a large lost investment. Try canning, smoking, salting and dehydrating for the bulk of your meat purchases.

An agrarian pantry must be replenished every year. The items in your pantry are purchased and stored under the assumption that they will be consumed within the next 12 months. Extra supplies should ideally be stored to make up for shortfalls caused by a poor harvest.

CANNING IS A COST-EFFECTIVE WAY TO BUILD YOUR PANTRY

For the frugal among us (and let's face it, prepping and frugality go together like peanut butter and jelly), canning can save you a lot of money. Home canning can be a great way to cost-effectively build your pantry for several reasons:

- you can buy in bulk
- you can take advantage of good sales
- you can buy in-season produce at better prices than off-season produce
- it costs less to put together canned meals than it does to buy processed foods
- you don't risk losing your stockpile to power outages like you would with your freezer

Thrifty Canning Tips

If the purpose of canning your own food is to save money, these tips can help!

DON'T GO SHOPPING JUST FOR A CANNING RECIPE; BE FLEXIBLE. It's okay to have a general idea of what you want to can, but if you have recipes that require specific ingredients beyond your pantry basics, you may end up spending a lot of money. For example, one day I went to a garden exchange and swapped some money and home-canned goodies for other people's surplus produce. When I got the items home, I looked at my bounty and decided what to make based on that. Had I gone to the store or market specifically looking for certain things, I would have spent far more. Be flexible when canning and learn to adapt the ingredients you have on hand.

FILL YOUR CANNER. If you only have enough ingredients for five jars of whatever you're making but your canner holds seven jars, fill the other two jars with beans (see Chapter 11). You'll be using the same amount of electricity or gas whether the canner is full or not.

BUY CHEAP AND GET CREATIVE. Recently, I went to a local orchard that had a huge sale on just-picked pears. Half bushels were on sale for $9. And it got even better—they were buy one, get one free! When you get a bounty like this, try to can the food in a way that provides you with some variety, instead of simply canning them all the same way.

COOK IN BULK AND CAN YOUR LEFTOVERS. The holidays can supply enormous amounts of food for your home canning endeavors. Also, as the weather cools off, make double batches of chili, soups, and stews, and put the leftovers into jars for later use (see Chapter 14).

Are you sold on canning as a way to stock your pantry yet? Read on, and I'll show you exactly how it's done.

THE HEALTHY CANNER'S MANIFESTO

A lot of people look at my canning projects and they shake their heads. "Why would you work that hard when you can just go to the grocery store?"

The list of reasons is long and distinguished.

I DON'T WANT TO SERVE FOOD-LIKE SUBSTANCES. I don't want food that has been concocted in a factory after being created by chemists who throw around words like "mouthfeel" and "sodium ethyl parahydroxybenzoate." I don't want to eat something that was chemically modified to taste like a different item, all to give a higher profit margin to Kraft or Kellogg's.

I DON'T WANT TO SERVE GENETICALLY MUTATED ORGANISMS. I don't want anything that was created in a petri dish at the labs of Monsanto, which infects more than 80 percent of food in the grocery store aisles. Many of the foods at the grocery store, even those in the produce aisle, are the result of a genetically sterilized seed. Corn and soy products are especially prone to modifications. These foods were altered to contain pesticides and mutations that allow them to grow bigger, faster, and more brightly colored. GMO foods were not thoroughly tested before being rushed to the market by Monsanto in their desire to create a world food monopoly. In independent studies,[1] laboratory animals that are fed a GMO diet develop multiple organ failure, sterility, greater allergic responses, high rates of offspring mortality, and premature death.

I CAN'T AFFORD TO HIT THE HEALTH FOOD STORE FOR EVERY BITE OF FOOD. These stores come to mind for most people when they think about organic or natural foods. But for most of us, specialty stores are financially out of reach. I can save money by getting locally grown foods when they are in season, cleaning them carefully, and preserving them for the winter ahead. This allows room in my budget for weekly grocery items like organic hormone-free milk.

EATING SEASONALLY PROVIDES NUTRITIONAL BENEFITS. I grow as much organic produce as I can on my small lot. I supplement what I grow with produce from a couple of local farms, where I have been lucky enough to forge a relationship with the farmers. Our food does not come from thousands of miles away, where it is picked while green and left to ripen in a box. It is picked and home-processed at the peak of its freshness as often as possible, which lets us conserve as many nutrients as we can for the winter ahead.

I EAT HUMANELY RAISED MEAT. I refuse to consume the growth hormones, antibiotics, and other medications that are given to factory-farmed animals. I spend a little bit more money and buy our meats in bulk from a local Mennonite butcher shop or a farmer that I know personally. They do not use any chemicals on their animals and the livestock is fed what livestock naturally eats—grass, hay, bugs, and seeds. Furthermore, the animals are

---

1   http://www.organiclifestylemagazine.com/doctors-against-gmos-hear-from-those-who-have-done-the-research

farmed humanely, reducing hormones like cortisol that are released when any animal is under stress.

HOME-CANNED FOOD IS THE FASTEST "FAST FOOD" AROUND. By preserving entire meals in jars, I can get a healthy and delicious meal on the table in a fraction of the time it would take to drive to a McDonald's and get the food home. Quite literally, a pot of homemade soup is steaming in a bowl in less than five minutes.

During the growing season, the work that I put in to cooking the food that will last us for the rest of the year probably requires less hands-on time than it would if I were producing the same meals throughout the year, one meal at a time. The reason for this is that I produce eight to sixteen meals at a time. Altogether, this consumes about two hours of preparation time and two hours of inactive processing time, when I can do other things. That is an average 20 minutes per meal, and half of that time is *not* spent in the kitchen.

I DON'T HAVE TO RELY ON THE POWER GRID TO KEEP MY FOOD FRESH. Tons of food—literally tons—is thrown out every year due to power outages. Most people stash meat and vegetables in their freezers, which is great as long as the power is up and running.

Canning might not be for everyone. It might not be for every meal. But as someone who firmly believes that our nutritional choices are the basis for our overall long-term physical and mental health, as the parent of a child with allergies and chemical sensitivities, and as an activist who refuses to support the food monopoly and toxic practices of companies like Monsanto and Dow Chemical, I have chosen along with my family to take the old-fashioned, healthy route to a pantry full of food.

CHAPTER 2

Food and Food Safety

If you've never canned before, you need to know the basics first. When you purchase your canning gear, be sure to thoroughly read the instructions. If you are new to this, you'll refer to this section of the book again and again while you get the hang of your new skill, so go ahead and fold down the corners of the pages that you find important. If your instruction manual disagrees with anything I say here, the instruction manual wins, as the instructions I provide are based on my own equipment.

With these types of recipes, it's very difficult to predict what the yield will be. The recipes aim for a canner load of six or seven jars, but there are a lot of variables, like these:

- the density of your fruits and vegetables
- the cooking duration
- the temperature and humidity conditions in your kitchen
- the weather on the day that you're canning
- the altitude where you're canning
- the different varieties of fruits and vegetables

You get the idea. It's difficult to really set your heart on a specific yield, so many of these recipes don't even try to predict the amount you'll end up with. I'll provide an estimate where possible and suggest a jar size where it makes sense, but when you are canning in a prepper-type situation, you're using up the food that you have on hand. Often, these quantities will not come in nice, neat, carefully weighed bushels. In any preparedness situation, adaptability is key.

SAFETY TIP: BEWARE OF BOTULISM

Every recipe in the book will tell you whether you should use a water bath canner or pressure canner. Water bath canning is *only* for high-acid foods like fruits and pickles. For everything else, you should use a pressure canner.

This is because of the risk of botulism. The absolute scariest part of canning is the thought that you might preserve your food incorrectly and subject your family to the risk of botulism.

Botulism isn't very common. Over the past 10 years, fewer than 300 cases were reportedly due to home-canned food. The percentages are on your side, particularly if you process your food carefully and according to USDA guidelines.

Botulism is caused by a germ called *Clostridium botulinum*. It lives in soil and thrives in an environment that is moist and free of oxygen, so canned food is the perfect medium in which it can thrive.

This toxin can cause a serious, life-threatening emergency with even a few bites of food.[2] Some of the symptoms of botulism are:

- double vision
- blurred vision
- drooping eyelids
- slurred speech
- difficulty swallowing

---

2   http://www.cdc.gov/features/homecanning

- dry mouth

- muscle weakness

When in Doubt, Throw It Out!

There are other ways home-canned food can be contaminated. If there is any doubt in your mind about whether your food is safe, discard it safely where it won't be eaten by humans or animals. (Pets can also die from botulism.)

Here are some warning signs that your canned food might be spoiled:

- a container that is swollen, bulging, misshapen, or leaking

- a container that looks cracked or damaged

- an eruption of liquid or foam when the jar is opened

- a bad smell

- discoloration

- visible mold

For the love of all things cute and fluffy, don't taste questionable food to see if it's okay. When in doubt, throw it out. It's not worth your life, and if you are consuming this food during a preparedness emergency, you may not have access to medical care.

I know all of the warnings about botulism are scary. It's scary stuff! That's why I get so aggravated when people say that a pressure canner is unnecessary. I get emails all the time from people who tell me things like this: "My Great Grandma Ida always processed her meat and green beans in a water bath canner for just three hours, and she lived to be 117 years old."

Anecdotes are not viable justifications for taking risky shortcuts. My granny did things like that too. She also didn't put her babies in car seats and did all sorts of other stuff that we don't do any longer. As recently as 30 years ago, folks didn't put their children in car seats. Most kids survived, but there were a few that bulleted through the front windshield.

We now possess the capability to make things safer than did our ancestors. If you have the ability and the equipment to avoid any risk of botulism, isn't your family worth the effort? Maybe they didn't have the equipment to do these things a century ago, but we have it now. Think how awful you would feel if your spouse or child died or suffered permanent physical damage because of something you fed them against standard advice.

To use a water bath canner for low-acid foods like meat and vegetables is to risk the lives of your family. It's that simple, and it's not worth the risk. We get to have the best of both worlds: old-fashioned skills combined with modern food science. Take advantage of them both.

Now that the botulism lecture is out of the way, let's move on and discuss canning practices that are safe and healthy.

BEST PRACTICES FOR CLEANING FRUITS AND VEGETABLES

While I would love for every bite we consume to be organic and fresh from the garden, budgetary restrictions don't always allow for that. Furthermore, even USDA-certified organic produce (particularly orchard fruits) might have an application of antibiotics. Organic veggies might even have some toxins because of spraying from nearby farms.

Of course, just because something isn't labeled organic doesn't necessarily mean it's slathered in chemicals. Many people don't realize the high price of becoming certified organic—it literally costs tens of thousands of dollars. Because of the price, a lot of local produce is traditionally grown and pesticide free but is not certified organic. It helps to purchase produce from local farms and to have a good relationship with a few favorite farmers. This way, you can quiz them about what, if anything, is sprayed on the goodies before you bring them home.

So what can you do about those fruits and veggies that do get sprayed? Apples, for example, can have more than 48 different pesticides on them, according to a report by the Environmental Working Group.[3] You can clean off more than 95 percent of pesticides if you are diligent in your process.

---

3   http://www.cbsnews.com/news/apples-top-list-for-pesticide-contamination/

I use the process below for cleaning all of our food before consuming or preserving it. Not only does it remove pesticides and traces of fertilizer, it also removes plain old ordinary dirt.

1. Put 1 cup of baking soda and some all-natural dish soap into a sink full of hot water. Use cool water for more delicate produce like berries or lettuce.

2. Allow your produce to soak in the solution for about 20 minutes. An alarming white film of gunk may rise to the top of the sink.

3. Drain the sink and rinse the produce. Rinse hearty produce under running water. For delicate produce, scrub your sink clean, fill it with fresh water, and swish the produce around in the clean water to rinse it.

4. Use a cloth and scrub the outside of thick-skinned, firm produce. Allow delicate produce to drain in a colander.

5. If you are still able to see a film or if the rinse water is cloudy, clean out your sink with white vinegar and repeat until your rinse water is clear.

The process is a bit time-consuming, but if you are putting in the effort to home-can so that your family has wholesome, delicious food, it's worthwhile to make certain your produce is as pristine as you can make it.

What Not to Can

There are some things that you should never can because, according to the food scientists at the USDA,[4] it simply cannot be done safely:

- barley
- butter
- milk
- cheese
- cornstarch
- cruciferous vegetables, unless pickled

---

4 http://nchfp.uga.edu/questions/FAQ_canning.html

- eggs

- flour of any type

- grains

- oats

- pasta

- purees

- rice

- summer squash and zucchini, unless pickled

CHAPTER 3

Canning 101

Preppers tend to think in worst-case scenarios. Because of this, we like to have everything on hand that we might possibly need in the event that we can't just run to the store to pick up a forgotten item.

If you are canning for preparedness' sake, you'll want to stock up on some particular supplies. The amount of supplies you'll need will be based on the size of your family, how much food you go through, and what you intend to can.

JARS

Our family of three uses about 400 jars per year for our canning projects and keeps about 100 extra just in case. These jars are ready to be reused as soon as they are washed.

I purchase name-brand jars, like Ball, because I've found that the cheaper jars are more likely to shatter during pressure canning, and that creates a heckuva mess, let me tell you. I have had excellent luck finding name-brand jars at thrift stores and yard sales. Be sure to run your finger over the rim of each jar when buying second hand. You want to feel for little nicks or chips that will keep your jars from sealing properly. Also, flip them over and inspect the bottoms for hairline cracks.

RINGS

Most of the time when you buy jars, they come with rings. I remove the rings before putting full jars into storage so I don't require as many rings as I do jars. Of course, if you're filling your jars with water when they aren't filled with food, you'll want to keep more rings on hand.

LIDS

I purchase lids (also known as flats) by the case and always keep at least four hundred on hand to sustain us throughout the year, though generally I have something closer to a two-year supply. Be sure to have lids for both regular and wide-mouth jars, if you use both kinds. Try to keep your lids at a moderate temperature year round. If they get too hot, the adhesive will be gummy ahead of time and may fail to seal. If they get too cold, the adhesive will be brittle and may fail to seal.

I avoid the cheap generic lids, especially for pressure canning. I have a higher rate of failure with those. I recommend Ball lids, which are BPA free.

Reusable Lids

"But what about reusable lids?" In principle, reusable lids should be a prepper's best friend. We love stuff that we can use over and over and never replace, right?

I have a confession. A non-prepperly confession. I have tried reusable lids, and I really, really didn't like them. I found that they were a bit more difficult to use because you have to make sure the stars are aligned, pray, sprinkle in the tears of a Tibetan maiden, and can only at midnight. Well, not really, but you get the general idea. There are many steps to using reusable lids, and everything must be perfect.

It's also unclear how safe these lids are, especially those of the Tattler brand. For example, *The Natural Canning Resource Book* by Lisa Rayner noted that the National Center for Home Food Preservation "documented higher levels of seal failure rates on Tattler lids" compared to other brands. Further studies have shown that many compounds, including alcohol, acids, chlorine, and sunlight can break down the plastic in the lids, which means that the plastic can leach into your food.

These lids also allow oxygen to survive in the headspace. Because the lid is largely inflexible and is only sealed after processing because of the way the band is tightened, it's tough to guarantee that all oxygen has been flushed out of the headspace; compare this with metal lids, where the vacuum itself is what creates the seal. This could create conditions where it is possible for nasty microorganisms to grow. As a precaution, I'll only use my current Tattler lids for processing high-acid foods like fruit.

Please use your own judgment when deciding which kind of lids will be best for your family.

CANNING SALT

I stock up on vast amounts of canning salt, also known as pickling salt. It's a preservative and an integral part of canning. It doesn't contain anti-caking additives, which can make canning liquid turn murky, or iodine, which can discolor fruits and veggies. You can also use kosher salt or sea salt, but keep in mind that sea salt is measured differently than canning salt. Take care not to overdo it.

SUGAR

Sugar, like salt, is a preservative, and it has a place in even the healthiest diet. You can purchase sugar in bulk and repackage it to last for a very, very long time. The key is to keep out moisture and bugs.

My favorite is turbinado sugar. Sucanat crystals are pure and unprocessed, but turbinado takes it a step further. The crystals are washed in a centrifuge to remove the surface molasses. This reduces the mineral content but makes turbinado sugar appropriate for recipes that call for white sugar.

When I have a recipe that calls for brown sugar, I turn to muscovado sugar. Muscovado is a very dark, unrefined sugar that has the highest molasses content of the natural sugars. It has an incredibly rich flavor and a texture like moist beach sand.

I primarily store organic, less processed sugar for my stockpile, although I do have a stash of inexpensive cane sugar stocked away just in case I run out of the good stuff. If you go with a less expensive sugar, cane sugar is the best option. If it doesn't say "cane sugar" on the package, it is most likely beet sugar. There's nothing inherently wrong with sugar made from beets, but sugar beets are usually genetically modified.[5] If you don't have an issue with GMOs, this won't affect your decision—this information is for those who are trying to avoid them.

Although it isn't genetically modified, that doesn't mean that non-organic cane sugar is actually a *good* option. It is often doused in Roundup (a brand of glyphosate) at harvest time to make certain the cane dies down evenly, increasing the yield. My suggestion? Go organic if you can.

LEMON JUICE

Unless you live in a place where lemons and limes grow, you could have difficulty getting a hold of lemon juice in a long-term disaster. Stock up on the plastic squeeze bottles of lemon juice, which will last for about a year, according to the labels. Lemon juice is an essential ingredient for many things you will be canning. Keep in mind that they are often preserved with sulfites, which some people can't tolerate. To make sure your lemon juice is good after a longer period of time, do *not* add it directly to your recipe. Put some in a little dish. Make sure it isn't murky and that it still smells OK. Dip your finger in and take a little taste. If it doesn't pass any of those three tests, discard it and use citric acid instead.

---

5   http://www.non-gmoreport.com/articles/jun08/sugar_beet_industry_converts_to_gmo.php

ASCORBIC/CITRIC ACID

This is not usually my first choice when canning, but I do stash away vitamin C tablets for the purpose of being able to add them to canning recipes if lemon juice is unavailable. Use six 500-milligram tablets per gallon of product or liquid.[6] You can also purchase citric acid or ascorbic acid on its own. The cheap citric acid is made from genetically modified mold (yuck!), so go with an organic source. You can often find a better quality citric acid where cheese-making supplies are sold.

VINEGAR

I keep both white vinegar and apple cider vinegar on hand in large quantities. Vinegar is a preservative, so it's safe to say that it will stay fresh on your pantry shelves almost indefinitely.[7]

The other bonus to vinegar is that you can make it yourself, often from food scraps that would otherwise be thrown away. However—and this is important—if you make your own vinegar, you must test the pH if you want to use it for canning. The safety of most canning recipes is based on the acidity levels of commercial vinegar. All you need to do this is grab a pack of inexpensive pH strips.[8] You'll want a pH of 2.4 or lower, because the lower the pH, the higher the acidity level is.

JAR PREP

Your preserved food is only as sanitary as the vessels you store it in. For some items, you will need to sanitize your jars, rings, and flats.

Some folks get really stressed out about this. Please keep in mind that you are not performing open-heart surgery. Nearly all canning recipes have to be processed for more than 10 minutes, which, in conjunction with the pre-sterilization you have performed, should keep your food safe and

---

6 http://nchfp.uga.edu/how/can_01/ascorbic_acid.html

7 http://www.eatbydate.com/other/condiments/how-long-does-vinegar-last

8 http://www.culturesforhealth.com/learn/kombucha/testing-acidity-strength-vinegar

healthy. In fact, the National Center for Home Preservation[9] recently said that it's *unnecessary* to sanitize the jars of foods that are going to be processed for 10 minutes or longer.

Because I store my jars outside in a shed, I do generally sanitize them by running them through the dishwasher. If you want to sanitize your jars or if your canning process will last less than 10 minutes, there are several methods for doing so.

The Dishwasher Method

If you have a dishwasher, this is the easiest method. Just run the sanitizing cycle right before you begin canning. The dishwasher will keep the jars hot until you are ready to fill them. The heat from the dishwasher will also make the rubber on the jar lid more pliable and ready to seal.

The Water Bath Canner Method

Assuming that your jars are clean and all you need to do is sanitize them, you can use your water bath canner for this.

1. Place them on the rack in the canner.

2. Pour in enough water to go over the opening of the jars and fill them.

3. Bring the canner to a boil and allow it to boil for 10 minutes.

4. Use your jar lifter and remove the jars, placing them upside down on a towel or drying rack to drain.

> **TIME SAVING HINT:** Reuse the hot water for canning once the jars are filled and lidded.

The Oven Method

You can also use your oven to sanitize your jars.

1. Preheat your oven to 225°F.

---

9   http://nchfp.uga.edu/how/can_01/sterile_jars.html

2. Place your jars in a roasting pan and slide them into the oven for at least 20 minutes.

3. Turn off the heat, but leave the jars in there until they are ready to be packed.

WARNING: This is kind of a "duh," but I'll say it anyway! The jars will be hotter than heck when you take them out of the oven, so take care not to burn yourself when filling them and placing them in the canner!

Sanitizing the Lids

It wouldn't do to put all that effort into making sure your jars are clean and then top them off with unsanitized lids!

1. In a small saucepan, bring enough water to a simmer to cover your lids and rings. Do not bring the lids to a rolling boil, as this could damage the sealing compound.

2. Keep the lids in the hot water and remove them with sanitized tongs or a lid lifter (a cool little magnetic wand) when you are ready to put them on the jars.

Breathe…remember, this isn't surgery. You're going to be processing your jars in boiling water, too!

WATER BATH CANNING

Water bath canning is a safe method for preserving high-acid foods. Some examples of foods that can be canned in a water bath are:

- jams and jellies
- fruit
- applesauce
- pickles
- tomato products

For water bath canning, you must have the following tools:

- big canning pot
- rack or folded towel
- jar lifter
- jar funnel
- jars
- lids
- rings

These items are the minimum tools you need for canning properly and safely. There are all sorts of other gadgets out there, like items that help you measure headspace and lid lifters with a little magnet on the end, but if you have the above items, you are ready to can!

Step-by-Step Water Bath Canning

While your product is on the stove, bubbling merrily away, follow these steps.

1. **Wash your jars, lids, and rings**. If you have a dishwasher, you can wash them in the dishwasher. The heat from it is enough to sanitize everything. If you are processing for longer than 10 minutes, you'll be golden. If not, you need to use one of the sanitation methods recommended previously. You can also add 10 minutes to your processing time in the water bath, but this can affect the quality of your product. Personally, I'm notoriously lazy and use the dishwasher.

2. **Prepare your canner**. Place your canner on the stove or burner and place the rack or folded towel on the bottom of your canner. Fill your canner with water, leaving about 3 to 5 inches at the top to allow for room for your filled jars. Bring your water to a boil. Because it takes forever and a day to bring that much water to a boil, I generally get it started while I am prepping my food.

3. **Fill your jars**. Line up your jars on a heatproof surface near the stove. You can place a towel on the counter to protect it from the hot, filled jars. Using the funnel, ladle your prepared product into the jars, leaving the recommended amount of headspace.

4. **Put on your lids**. With a dry, clean dishtowel, carefully wipe the lip of the filled jars to remove any residue. Place the lids on each jar, then tighten the rings by hand. You don't have to use much torque on them. The rings simply hold the lids in place until they seal.

5. **Place your jars in the canner**. With your handy-dandy jar lifter, place the closed jars carefully into the canner. Put them in gently because as you know, boiling water hurts when it splashes on you. Be careful not to let the jars touch each other because they could break, and that makes a big mess you won't want to deal with. Make sure the lids are all completely submerged. They don't have to be under by inches, just covered.

6. **Process the jars**. Put the lid back on your canner and bring the water to a rolling boil. Don't start clocking your processing time until the water is at a full boil. Then just leave the jars in the water bath for the time required by your recipe.

7. **Remove the jars from the canner**. Using your jar lifter, carefully remove the jars from the boiling water. Tip the jars to the side to allow the hot water to drip off the top. Then place the jars on your towel or heatproof surface.

8. **Leave 'em alone**! Allow 12 to 24 hours for the jars to cool and seal. You will hear musical "pop," "plink," and "ping" noises as the jars seal in the cool air; that is the lid getting sucked down and forming a seal to the lip of the jar.

9. **Remove the rings**. When you are ready to store the jars, you can remove the rings. This keeps your rings from rusting because of moisture trapped between the metal ring and the jar.

10. **Test the seals**. Test the seal by pushing down with your finger. If it pops back and forth, it is not sealed. Another way to check is by picking up your jar by the lid. It should remain firmly adhered to the rim of the jar. If it is not properly sealed, put it in the

refrigerator and use the unsealed product in the next few weeks. You can also reprocess your food, as long as it's done within 24 hours.[10] Use a new lid if you do this.

11. **Put it away**. Store your sealed little gems in a cool, dark place. It's okay to peek in and admire them from time to time.

PRESSURE CANNING

Low-acid foods have to be preserved at higher temperatures than do high-acid foods. The low-acid environment welcomes the growth of bacteria like botulism, a form of food poisoning that can cause permanent nerve damage or even death. (Remember botulism from page 11?) The temperature must reach 240°F, which can only be achieved through steam under pressure. Pressure canning exceeds the temperature of water bath canning, getting your product into the safety zone that prevents the possibility of botulism. All vegetables (except for tomatoes, which are botanically a fruit), meats, seafood, and poultry must be preserved in a pressure canner.

I'll be honest—I was utterly terrified the first time I used my pressure canner. I was certain I was going to blow up my kitchen. This fear was backed up when I put the regulator (that little black round thing you see on the top) on askew, which led to my screaming and dropping the regulator, and the canner's making a gosh-awful whistling noise.

But after successfully pressure canning a couple of times, I'm actually equally as comfortable using this method as I am using the water bath method. Some recipes can be made using either canner, but when it's an option I nearly always choose the pressure canner because it is far faster for those recipes.

Pep talk is over—let's pressure can!

For pressure canning, you need:

• pressure canner with valves, seals, and gauges

• rack or folded towel

---

10   http://nchfp.uga.edu/questions/FAQ_canning.html#1

- jar lifter

- jar funnel

- jars

- lids

- rings

Like water bath canning, you can get all the fancy gadgets if you want to, but the ones listed above are the essentials.

The instructions in this book are for a dial gauge canner. If you happen to have a weighted gauge canner, you can only apply pressure during canning at either 5, 10, or 15 pounds. If the pressure required for canning a certain food does not exactly match any of these values, go up to the next highest pressure. For example, if the recipe calls for 11 pounds of pressure (PSI), then use the 15-pound weight setting.

Step-by-Step Pressure Canning

One thing you will notice about pressure canning is that it is actually very similar to water bath canning. Differences are really only related to the equipment. Once you have learned to use your pressure canner correctly, you will find it every bit as easy as water bath canning.

Remember to always check the instructions on your individual canner. If there is a discrepancy between what you read here and in the instructions, go with the instructions that came with your product.

1. **Wash your jars, lids, and rings**. You'll be processing them for long enough and at hot enough temperatures that sanitizing them is unnecessary.

2. **Prepare your canner**. Place your canner on the stove or burner. Place your rack or folded towel in the bottom of your canner and add about 3 inches of water to the canner. Most pressure canners have a line to which they should be filled with water. In pressure canning, it is not necessary for the water to cover the lids. At this point, you can turn the burner on low to begin warming the water, but don't bring it to a boil yet.

3. **Fill your jars**. Line up your jars on the counter near the stove. If the surface is not heatproof, place a towel on the counter first because the filled jars will be very hot. Ladle the prepared product into the jars using the funnel, leaving the headspace recommended in your recipe.

4. **Put on your lids**. With a dry, clean dishtowel, carefully wipe the lip of the filled jars, making sure to get any residue of food off. Place the lids on each jar, then tighten the rings—you don't have to really twist too hard, as the lids will seal in the canner. If you are canning a fatty food, you can use a cloth dampened with vinegar to remove any fat on the rim that might prevent a good seal.

5. **Place your jars in the canner**. Be careful not to let the jars touch because not only could they could break when they bump together in the boiling water, but in pressure canning, the steam must be able to completely surround the jars.

6. **Build steam in the canner**. Before putting the lid on the canner, check the vent pipe to be sure it is clear. Place the lid firmly on the canner, latching it as per the specifics of your canner, and increase the heat to bring the water to a boil. At this point, steam should be coming out the vent pipe. Reduce the heat until a moderate amount of steam is coming steadily out of the pipe for 10 minutes. The purpose of this is to release the air and build up the steam inside the canner. If you don't give it the whole 10 minutes, your canner will not build pressure. As patience is not my strong point, I learned this from experience.

7. **Close the vent**. After exhausting the steam for 10 minutes, either close the petcock valve or place the weighted regulator on the vent pipe, depending on your canner. When I place the regulator on, I always put a dishtowel around my hand, because steam is *hot*. It sometimes makes a loud, high-pitched noise when you are putting the regulator on. Don't be alarmed by the various rattling, whistling, and bubbling noises. Pressure canning is loud business.

8. **Pressurize the canner**. Turn up the heat on the burner and wait until the gauge has reached the desired pressure. (Pressure will

differ based on altitudes and recipes—see page 29 for altitude adjustments). This usually takes three to five minutes. Note that if you lose pressure while processing, you must start the processing time from the beginning.

9. Adjust the heat to maintain the pressure. This part takes practice. Monitor your canner while it is processing to be sure the pressure is maintained. I have found that turning the dial on my electric stove to somewhere around four keeps my pressure between 10 to 12 pounds quite steadily.

10. Release the pressure. When your processing time is over, it is time to release the pressure. It couldn't be easier. Turn off the burner. Take the canner off the burner and put it on a heatproof surface. Walk away. Allow the canner to return to room temperature and release pressure naturally. Don't try to cool it down faster—that is how people get hurt while pressure canning. The pressure is completely reduced when the air vent/cover lock and overpressure plug have dropped, and when no steam escapes when the pressure regulator is tilted. The gauge, if your canner has one, should be completely at zero. This entire process can take more than 45 minutes and must not be rushed!

11. Open the vent. When the pressure is gone, open the petcock or remove the weighted regulator. If the regulator doesn't want to come off, there is likely still some pressure in the canner. Don't force it—walk away for another 15 minutes. Once the vent is open, leave the canner for another two to five minutes.

12. Remove the jars from the canner. Use potholders to protect your hands while you unlatch the lid of your pressure canner. Very carefully, remove the lid from canner, turning it away from you so that you are not burned by the steam that will rush out. Using your jar lifter, carefully remove the jars from the canner one by one. Then place the jars on your towel or heatproof surface.

13. Allow 12 to 24 hours for the jars to cool and seal. Let the jars stand overnight in a draft-free place where they will not be moved or bumped. Jars that are sealed properly will bubble away on the counter for quite some time after they have been removed

from the pressure canner. You will hear a musical "pop" as the jars seal in the cool air—that is the sound of the lid getting sucked down and forming a seal on the jar. When you are ready to store the jars, you can remove the rings. This will keep your rings from rusting because of moisture trapped between the metal ring and the jar.

14. Test the seal by pushing down with your finger. If it pops back and forth, it is not sealed. Another way to check is by picking the jar up by the lid. The lid should remain firmly adhered to the rim of the jar. If it is not properly sealed, put it in the refrigerator and use the unsealed product within the next few weeks. You can also reprocess your food as long as it's done within 24 hours. Use a new lid if you do this.

15. Store your jars in a cool, dark place.

ALTITUDE ADJUSTMENT

My canning friends, sometimes we have to look at our situations and say to ourselves, "I need an altitude adjustment."

It's time to talk science, which so much of canning is. At sea level and up to 1,000 feet above sea level, water boils at 212°F. However, once you get above the 1,000-foot mark, the changes in atmospheric pressure mean that the boiling point is actually *lower* than 212°F.

ALTITUDE (FEET)	TEMPERATURE AT WHICH WATER BOILS
0 (Sea Level)	212°F
2,000	208°F
4,000	204°F
6,000	201°F
8,000	197°F
10,000	194°F

Because of these differences in boiling point, we must add extra processing time in order to make our food safe. It simply isn't worth the risk to miss a few minutes of canning time, so learn your altitude and adjust your times accordingly. I had to re-calculate all of the times and pressures that I had been using when I moved from sea level to my new home 3,000 feet the mountains.

Water Bath Canning Adjustments

Food safety requirements state that the goodies inside your jars should reach 212°F when water bath canning, and if they don't, you have to add to your processing time in order to make your preserved food safe.

For water bath canning, add two-and-a-half minutes of processing time for every 1,000 feet above sea level. Use the following chart as a reference on how to increase processing time based on your elevation.

ADJUSTMENTS FOR WATER BATH CANNING

ELEVATION	ADDITIONAL TIME
1,000–2,999	+5 minutes
3,000–5,999	+10 minutes
6,000–7,999	+15 minutes
8,000–10,000	+20 minutes

Pressure Canning Adjustments

Pressure canning requires that your food reach 240°F. When pressure canning at higher altitudes, you need additional pressure as opposed to additional time.

The standard rule is to add 1 pound of pressure for every 1,000 feet above sea level. However, you will rarely ever adjust more than 5 pounds, regardless of your elevation.

For safety reasons, pressure canners should never be used above 17 pounds of pressure.

ADJUSTMENTS FOR PRESSURE CANNING

ELEVATION	ADDITIONAL PRESSURE
1,000–1,999	+ 1
2,000–3,999	+ 3
4,000–5,999	+5
6,000–7,999	+5
8,000–10,000	+5

For the recipes included in this book, times and pressures are given based on sea level altitudes, so use these charts to adjust according to your location.

CANNING IN A GRID-DOWN SITUATION

Power outages are one of the most common emergencies that we prep for. But in many homes, if the power goes out, so does the kitchen stove. If you have a refrigerator and freezer full of food that you want to preserve before it spoils, you're going to need a back-up plan for grid-down situations. Here are a few different methods. Choose one, and be sure to get enough fuel to be able to do a substantial amount of canning with.

In the event of a power outage, turn to Chapter 14 to learn about canning leftovers and the foods you have in your refrigerator, especially if you won't be able to eat everything before it goes bad. Once you're finished with that, begin methodically canning the contents of your freezer.

Gas Kitchen Stove

This is the most ideal back-up plan, because you'll be preserving food just like you would any other time and leaving less margin for error.

In my current home, the kitchen stove runs off of the same propane that runs the heater. In the event of a power outage, I will be able to can to my heart's content. We have two propane tanks, one of which is filled as soon as it is emptied while we switch over to the second tank. The only caveat is that some modern propane stoves ignite using a piezoelectric lighter, which means that they still want electricity to run. Manually igniting your gas stove may void the warranty. It's a good idea to test this ahead of time to see if your stove will light easily without power.

Outdoor Propane Burner

Before I had a gas kitchen stove, I used an outdoor propane burner, not only for emergency canning but sometimes to help keep the kitchen cool in the heat of the summer.

This burner has a low center of gravity and can support a very large stockpot or canning pot. It should have an attachment that allows it to be hooked up with the type of small propane tank you'd use for your gas barbecue. Mine is a Bayou Classic, and I've used it for both pressure canning and water bath canning.

Of course, there is whole list of warnings about burners:

- You don't want the kind of burner that is designed for deep-frying turkeys. Those get way too hot and will warp your canner.

- Be sure that you put your burner on a very stable, level surface that is out of the wind. A canning pot that tips over could cause very serious burns.

- Choose a burner with a very low profile for more stability.

- Keep kids, pets, and irresponsible or intoxicated adults far away from your burner when you are canning.

- Check whether the manufacturer says that the burner will work for canning. Some burners will not maintain an even heat. (The Bayou Burners manufacturer recommends the product for outdoor canning use.[11])

Wood Stove/Fireplace/Outdoor Fire Pit

These are less than ideal. While I haven't personally canned on a fireplace, I did experiment with pressure canning on my wood stove, and I had to use a vast amount of fuel to keep my pot at the correct pressure. You

---

11   http://www.bayouclassicdirect.com/propane-burnerscookers

need to attend to the fire almost constantly to ensure that the pressure does not drop, which would cause you to have to start all over again. If you are doing this indoors, even in the winter, your house will be about a thousand degrees. I can only assume that a fireplace or fire pit would offer similar challenges. Again—it *is* possible, but it is far from ideal.

Outdoor Wood Stove

If you have an outdoor kitchen set up, you may have a better set-up for off-grid canning. If you have a stove with grates you can raise or lower, you will have a lot more success than with canning over an open fire. You'll still need tons of firewood, and according to the website An American Homestead,[12] it's *not* a one-person job.

---

12   http://anamericanhomestead.com/10-tips-for-canning-over-a-wood-fire/

PART 2

Preserving the Basics

CHAPTER 4

Traditional Canning Tips and Recipes

This section of the book deals with preserving the basics. In the type of long-term sustainability scenario many of us are concerned about, being able to *preserve* the food you raise is every bit as important as being able to raise the food. The only way you'll make it through the time between growing seasons is by storing food, and canning is a method that will work for many different foods. Let's get started on the nitty gritty basics that will make up the backbone of your home-preserved food store!

CONDIMENTAL FARE

Chapters 5 through 7 will teach you how to can your own condiments. You can make the simplest fare tastier, more elegant, and even more nutritious with the right condiment. I'm not talking about squirting ketchup on a burger—I'm talking about a mouth-watering relish made of garden vegetables, a surprisingly luscious fruit salsa, a decadent homemade jam, or a sweet-n-savory chutney that you can use to turn relatively bland prepper pantry items into instant gourmet.

Nearly all of condiments in this book have an acidity level that allows for water bath canning, unless otherwise noted. For that reason, I've put it first in the book. Jams and condiments are a wonderful, immediately gratifying way to get your feet wet with canning.

Having shelves full of chutneys and relishes will add a boost of nutrition and flavor to your meals. Furthermore, many chutneys are of the "kitchen sink" variety, which means that you can use up those odds and ends of produce that are not quite enough to make a full batch based on any single item. When your garden is producing more than you can eat, consider preserving some leftovers as condiments to add to the variety on your groaning pantry shelves. With your pantry full of jams and condiments, you can get your fancy on at any time!

THE NITTY GRITTY BASICS

Chapters 8 through 11 focus on the basic ingredients that make up most of the meals you'll be cooking. When you have fruit, vegetables, and meat in your pantry, you can combine these basics in untold ways to make delicious meals. Because these prepared foods have little in the way of seasoning, they will be adaptable to many different types of cuisine when they're needed.

Canned foods of this nature don't have an extremely long shelf life when compared with grains and dried beans. They are not meant to be in long-term storage. Rather, this process is a nod to our agrarian ancestors, who stored food each year to get them through to the next harvest plus a little extra, in case the harvest was poor. Home-canned food lasts for "at least a year"[13] according to the USDA, although some people maintain that the food is safe and tasty long after that time.

Generally, I can my produce all summer and fall. In the winter and spring, I can my meat. Doing it this way, I have a nice, rotating supply and I'm not doing everything at once.

---

13   http://nchfp.uga.edu/questions/FAQ_canning.html#5

TOMATO, TOMAHTO: AN IMPORTANT NOTE

Since you'll be using tomatoes in a lot of the recipes in this book, I wanted to give you some tips on how to handle them up front. Come back and reference this page every time a recipe calls for prepped tomatoes.

Get More Tomatoes

Here's my recommendation for your end-of-summer food preservation: you'll need 100 pounds of tomatoes. I can hear your shock from here: "100 pounds? Are you insane, Daisy?"

Get 100 pounds of tomatoes or more if you can. No other item of produce increases in nutrients when cooked and stored like tomatoes. Canning tomatoes is like loading your shelves with vitamins and tasty meals throughout the winter, when fresh, locally grown fruits and veggies are expensive and scarce.

I plant more tomatoes in my garden than anything else because we love them so much. You can often find tomatoes by the bushel for $1 to $2 per pound at your local farmer's market or, if your friends have an overabundance, you can barter for finished products.

Trust me. Get as many tomatoes as you can get your hands on, and you won't regret it.

Prepping Your Tomatoes

Everyone loves tomato season, or, as I like to call it, "Make Your Kitchen Look Like a Crime Scene" season!

I'm not gonna lie—there is nothing messier than a bushel of tomatoes getting jarred. It's a fair bit of work to process your own tomato products, but the intensely flavored results make it all worthwhile.

These are some short cuts to speed along your tomato processing procedures.

Mess-Free Tomato Peeling

Lots of people already know this little trick but it bears repeating, especially when you are looking at an entire bushel of those bad boys!

1. Begin boiling a pot of water on the stove. At the same time, prep a large bowl with very icy water.

2. Slide tomatoes into the pot of boiling water for 1 to 2 minutes. You will know they are ready to come out because the skin will start to wrinkle up.

3. Use a slotted spoon to remove the tomatoes and drop them instantly into the ice bath, where you can leave them for as long as you need to.

4. Once the tomato is cool enough to touch, you can easily slide the skin off with your fingers.

This process also works like a charm on thin-skinned fruits like peaches, nectarines, and apricots.

Coring the Tomatoes

There's more than one way to skin a cat—er, core a tomato! You can simply use a paring knife and cut it out. Or, you can use an old-fashioned hand crank food mill that spits the bad stuff out one end and the good stuff out the other.

Turning Tomatoes into a Sauce-Like Consistency

You can turn your tomatoes into a sauce-like consistency in three different ways.

• Dump the whole mess of cored and peeled tomatoes into a big stockpot, as is or roughly chopped, and cook them down.

• Puree them by batches in a food processor or blender and then cook them down.

• Put them through the food mill, then cook them down in the stockpot.

For me, the choice relies on what I am making. For spaghetti sauces, I prefer the consistency of the tomatoes that come out of the food mill. If I'm making sauces, like ketchup or barbecue sauce, I prefer to use the food processor.

Consider your tomatoes officially prepped. From this point on, you'll be ready to proceed with your recipes!

CHAPTER 5

Jazz Things Up with Jams

One of the easiest things to can is jam or jelly. It is a quick water bath canning project that can be done in just a few hours and is quite satisfying. Learn how to make jam and you'll be able to supply your family with jam for the entire winter ahead.

The typical way to make jam is with boxed or bottled pectin. It's also possible to make jam without pectin (see page 44). Both methods are universal recipes, meaning you can follow the same set of instructions to make any type of jam. On page 46, you'll find a chart that provides specific instructions and processing times for different types of fruit.

HOW TO MAKE JAM WITH BOXED PECTIN

If you will be using boxed pectin to make your jam, here are the basic instructions for that process. The amounts of fruit, sugar, lemon juice, and pectin that you will be using will vary based on the recipe you are making; this is a general set of instructions for making jam with pectin. Note that pectin comes in different sized packages, so when in doubt, follow the instructions that come with your pectin.

1. Prep your fruit by washing it and cutting it up if necessary.

2. Smush your fruit. You can do this with a potato masher, food processor, blender, or food mill. For some fruits, I like to puree them for a smoother jam and for others, I like chunkier jam—it's up to personal preference.

3. In a small bowl, use a fork to mix ¼ cup of the sugar with one packet of pectin, unless the directions on your packet specify a different amount.

4. In a saucepan, add the fruit, lemon juice, and pectin together. Mix well.

5. Bring the mixture to a boil over medium heat, stirring frequently.

6. Once mixture is boiling, stir in the sugar and return to a boil for 1 minute.

7. Test your jam (see below).

8. Ladle the jam carefully into your awaiting jars, wipe the rims, and cap your jars with lids and rings.

9. Process in a hot water bath canner, according to the ingredients chart.

Jam Making Rule of Law: Always Test Your Jam!

Keep a spoon in the freezer. To test your jam, drip a bit of the hot jam into the spoon, which will allow it to quick cool. The consistency the jam will reach is the same consistency your finished product will have.

After testing, I nearly always end up adding another quarter to half package of pectin. I use the cheaper pectin to "top it up." Then, I return my jam mixture to a simmer for a couple of minutes and test again.

Omitting this step may result in a very tasty ice cream topping or waffle syrup, but not jam!

The Scoop on Pectin

For years when I made jam, I reached for a box of pectin from the store. But when I spent some time reading up on store-bought pectin, I was very unhappy to discover that the jams I'd been making for my family had been tainted with GMOs. I had unknowingly been contaminating my carefully-sourced fruit and pricey turbinado sugar with the very things I strive to avoid, and I hadn't even given it a second thought.

Most brands breathlessly exclaim "all natural pectin" or "made from real fruit." And this is true—pectin does originate from fruit. But don't be deceived. This misleading label makes it sound as though boxed pectin is nothing more than some powdered fruit.

Here are the ingredients from the box of pectin lurking in my canning cupboard:

- citric acid

- dextrose

- fruit pectin

Dextrose is generally made from cornstarch, the main ingredient in good old high-fructose corn syrup. And don't let anyone tell you that citric acid is "just vitamin C." It is derived from GMO mold (see page 20 for more on this). Plus, not only does store-bought pectin contain unsavory ingredients, but it is also very highly processed.

So, if you want to avoid GMOs and processed foods, what's a homemade-jam making mama to do?

Jam has been around for thousands of years. The first known book of jam recipes was written in Rome in the first century.[14] Since I'm pretty sure our ancestors didn't have those handy little boxes of Sure-Jel or Certo sitting in their pantries, I set out to learn how they made thick, delicious preserves to spread on their biscuits.

My first attempt at breaking up with the box was to make my own pectin with green apples. While I ended up with a tasty product, it wasn't really

---

14   http://www.purejam.com/History_of_Jam.htm

jam-like. It's possible, considering the time of year, that the apples were too ripe to allow this to work for me, but I assume that unripe apples were not always available in the past when people wanted to make jam from the currently ripe harvest.

I continued to read recipes and methods from days gone by. It soon became clear that adding pectin wasn't really necessary at all. In days past, the sugar and the fruit worked hand-in-hand to create the desired consistency.

I combined bits from a few different methods and finally came up with a jam that the entire family was happy with. In comparison with the boxed pectin jam, it doesn't gel quite as much, but after trying this jam, the texture of the others now seems slightly artificial to me. This produces a softer preserve with an incredibly intense fruit flavor. Also, when using this method, you don't get that layer of foam that you have to skim off the top like you do with the boxed pectin method.

The instructions for basic non-pectin jams are pretty much the same regardless of what jam you'll be making. You will only need to make minor modifications for different fruits.

When making non-pectin jams, you'll also wind up with a fantastic by-product. When you drain the fruit, the juice collected can be turned into a delicious syrup and processed at the same time as your jam. Your yield for this recipe will vary based on which fruit you use. See Basic Jam-Making Guidelines on page 46.

Pectin-Free Jam and Fruit Syrup

Makes approximately 6 (1-pint) jars

7 pounds (14 to 20 cups) fresh or frozen fruit

¼ cup lemon or lime juice

5 cups and 2 tablespoons sugar, divided

clean cotton fabric for draining (I used a flour sack towel. This will be permanently stained, so don't use something you want to keep pretty.)

1. Prepare your fruit. For berries, this means washing them, sorting them, and removing little leaves and twigs, as well as shriveled berries. Leave the odd green berry in, because less ripe fruit has more naturally occurring pectin than ripe fruit. For fruits like apples or peaches, this might mean blanching and peeling them, then removing the cores.

2. Mash, finely chop, or puree your fruit. I used a blender to puree half of the fruit, and a food processor to finely chop the other half. We prefer a slightly rough texture.

3. Pour your mixture into a large crock or non-reactive bowl, layering your fruit with 3 cups of sugar. I use the ceramic insert from my slow cooker for this.

4. Leave the fruit and sugar mixture in your refrigerator overnight. The juice from the fruit will combine with the sugar and form a slightly jelled texture. Some liquid will separate from the sugar and fruit.

5. The next day, line a colander with a piece of fabric. Place the colander into a pot to catch the liquid from the fruit and sugar mixture.

6. Pour your fruit and sugar mixture into the fabric-lined colander. Put this back in the refrigerator for at least an hour to drain. You can let it drain for longer with no ill effect; in fact, this will result in an even thicker jam.

7. When you're ready to make jam, scoop the fruit out of the fabric-lined colander and place it in a pot, leaving lots of extra space for liquid to evaporate. This helps it cook down faster.

8. The approximately 2 pints of liquid that you caught in the other pot will form the basis for your fruit syrup. Place that pot on the stove and bring it to a rolling boil. Add ¼ cup of sugar and a tablespoon of lemon juice per pint and reduce heat to a simmer. I like to add one big spoonful of jam to this to add a little texture to the syrup.

9. On another burner, bring your fruit and sugar mixture to a simmer, stirring frequently. Taste test and add up to two cups of additional sugar. After about an hour, the texture will have thickened. If you

still have a great deal of liquid, you can use a fabric-lined sieve to strain some more out. You can add this liquid to the syrup.

10. Fill sanitized jars with your finished products. Process the water bath canner according to the type of fruit you are canning (see Basic Jam-Making Guidelines below, and make adjustments for your altitude.

MAKING BASIC JAMS

While recipes are helpful if you are making a fancy jam with multiple ingredients, you don't actually need a recipe for basic jams. You can use this chart to figure out the water bath canner processing times and special instructions for whatever fruit you happen to have on hand. Remember to always adjust for altitude!

BASIC JAM-MAKING GUIDELINES		
FRUIT	SPECIAL INSTRUCTIONS	PROCESSING TIME
Apricot	Peel, slice in half to pit	5 minutes
Blackberry	optional step: mill to remove seeds	10 minutes
Blueberry	optional step: puree	7 minutes
Cherry	Pit with a cherry pitter, chop before cooking	10 minutes
Grape	Mill to remove seeds	10 minutes
Huckleberry	Check for stems	10 minutes
Peach	Peel, slice in half to remove pits	10 minutes
Plum	Slice in half to remove pits	5 minutes
Raspberry	Crush with a potato masher	10 minutes
Strawberry	Remove cores, mash with a potato masher	10 minutes

Blueberry Lemon Jam

This stuff is like the Muse of Jams. Everyone that has tried it has been struck with sudden inspiration:

"Oh my gosh, can you imagine this on pancakes?"

"Wow! What if you used it in shortbread thumbprint cookies?"

"This is just begging for some good English scones!"

You get the idea. You've gotta try it! Just a warning, though: if you choose to use a potato masher to smush your berries, you will find berries behind the fridge, under the stove, beside the sink—I've even found a couple in the bathroom! Those bad boys go everywhere.

Makes approximately 7 (1-pint) jars

7 to 8 pints fresh or frozen blueberries

4–5 cups sugar, to taste, separated

¾ cup lemon or lime juice, separated

1. Wash and sort your berries. Look out for the little woody stems that like to hide in the berries and create a sneaky, unpleasant texture in your finished product.

2. Smush your berries. I like to use my blender or food processor to puree the daylights out of them, but some people want more texture, in which case you could use a potato masher.

3. Pour your berries into a crock and layer them with 3 cups of the sugar. Top with ½ cup of lemon juice. Leave this in your fridge overnight.

4. The next day, place a fabric-lined colander in a bigger pot. Drain your berries and sugar mixture for at least an hour.

5. When you're ready to make jam, scoop the fruit out of the fabric-lined colander and place it in a pot, leaving lots of extra space to help it cook down faster.

6. Bring your fruit and sugar mixture to a simmer, stirring frequently. After about an hour, the texture will have thickened. If you still have a great deal of liquid, you can use a fabric-lined sieve to strain some more out.

7. Stir in ¼ cup of lemon or lime juice and 1 cup of sugar. Increase heat to bring mixture back to a simmer.

8. Optional: Use the 1 to 2 pints of liquid that you caught in the other pot as the basis for a fruit syrup. Place that on the stove and bring it to a rolling boil. Add ¼ cup of sugar and 1 tablespoon of lemon juice per pint, and reduce heat to a simmer. You can add one big spoonful of jam to add texture.

9. When it has reached the desired texture, ladle the jam carefully into your awaiting jars, wipe the rims, and cap your jars with lids and rings. If you made any, ladle the syrup into jars, too.

10. Lid your jars and process them in a water bath canner for 7 minutes, adjusting for altitude. After allowing your little gems of blueberry-lemon jam to cool, greedily hide them away so you don't have to share.

Dandelion Blossom Jam

If you are lucky enough to live in or visit an area that you are *absolutely certain* does not spray pesticides, you can join the bees and enjoy some dandelion nectar—except yours will be in the form of jam. So far, this jam has only been made successfully with added pectin. You'll be left with a topaz-toned honey-like substance that will give you a new understanding of the minds of bees.

Set forth on an expedition to pick dandelions. You only need the yellow flowers from the top of the dandelions; you can break them off right at the top of the stem. Pick 10 to 12 cups worth of blossoms. Your kids will think it is great fun initially, but then they'll get bored and you will have to pick the rest.

Makes approximately 6 (1-pint) jars

10 to 12 cups dandelion blossoms

2 tablespoons lemon juice

1 packet of pectin (size varies with brand)

4½ cups sugar

1. Prepare the blossoms by pinching them between your fingers and snipping off the green part with scissors.

2. Place the petals in a large glass bowl and cover them with 4 cups of boiling water. That's it for today! You're going to sleep while the petals brew up a golden yellow, room temperature dandelion tea.

3. The next morning, drain the tea through a coffee filter into another container. You should have 3 to 4 cups of dandelion tea.

4. Pour the strained tea into a saucepan and stir in the lemon juice.

5. Following the instructions on your pectin package, add the pectin and sugar to the contents of the saucepan. (See page 41 for instructions on using pectin for jam making.)

6. Test your jam. When the consistency is right, remove it from the heat and immediately ladle it into sanitized jars.

7. Lid your jars and process them in a water bath canner for 10 minutes, adjusting for altitude.

Spiced Cherry Amaretto Jam

Sadly, cherries are some of the most highly sprayed fruits out there, according to the Environmental Working Group's annual "Dirty Dozen" report.[15] I strongly recommend that you use organic cherries to make this jam. Bing cherries are especially delicious. If you must use non-organic cherries, wash your fruit well in a baking soda bath, then rinse well to get as much residue off as possible (see page 13 for more thorough instructions). Also note that unlike with most pectin-free recipes, cherries don't need to sit overnight or be drained of excess liquid.

Makes approximately 6 (1-pint) jars

4 pounds sweet cherries	1 teaspoon ground cinnamon
4½ cups sugar	½ teaspoon ground cloves
¼ cup amaretto	¼ teaspoon ground allspice
½ cup lemon juice	¼ teaspoon ground nutmeg
¼ teaspoon salt	

---

15 https://www.ewg.org/foodnews/dirty_dozen_list.php

1. Using a cherry pitter, remove the pits from the cherries.

2. In batches, roughly chop the cherries using your food processor.

3. Place the cherries into a saucepan and stir in sugar, amaretto, lemon juice, salt, and spices.

4. Bring the mixture to a boil, then reduce heat and simmer until you've reached the desired consistency.

5. Ladle the hot jam into sanitized pint jars, allowing ¼ inch of headspace.

6. Lid the jars and process in a water bath canner for 10 minutes, adjusting for altitude.

Ginger Peach Jam

It's like a taste of summer with a bite of spice! You will *not* want to share, so plan to make a second batch for gifts.

Peaches can be peeled just like tomatoes (see page 39). Blanch them for a minute in boiling water then drop them into ice water, and the skin will slide right off!

Makes approximately 6 (1-pint) jars

6 pounds peeled, chopped peaches

5 cups sugar, divided

2-inch piece fresh ginger, grated

1 teaspoon ground cinnamon

¼ cup lemon juice

1 teaspoon ground nutmeg

vanilla extract (optional)

1. Prep your peaches by blanching them in hot water, then dipping them in an ice bath to remove the peel. Remove the pit.

2. Mash or roughly puree the peaches. Layer them with 3 cups of sugar in a crock and place them in the fridge overnight.

3. Using a fabric-lined colander over a bowl, drain the puree for 3 hours.

4. In a large saucepan, bring drained peaches, ginger, cinnamon, lemon juice, and nutmeg to a boil. Reduce heat and simmer. (Smell that peachy spicy goodness? Mmmmm…hey—no tasting!)

5. Meanwhile, in another pot, simmer your peach juice with ¼ cup of sugar per pint. You can add a little vanilla extract to the syrup for a different flavor.

6. Add the remaining sugar to the jam, stir well, and simmer until it reaches the consistency you prefer.

7. When it reaches the consistency you like, ladle into your sanitized jars.

8. Process the jars in a water bath canner for 10 minutes, adjusting for altitude.

Slow Cooker Plum Butter

This incredibly simple, hands-off recipe requires practically no attention from the time you put it in the slow cooker until the time you put it in jars for canning! Meanwhile, it selflessly makes your home smell wonderful while you ignore it.

Makes approximately 8 (1-pint) jars

14 pounds plums	1 teaspoon ground nutmeg
4 cups sugar	2 tablespoons vanilla extract

1. Remove pesticides from the skins of the plums. Once they are clean, slice your plums in half, remove the stones, and toss them in the slow cooker.

2. Stir in the sugar and nutmeg.

3. Set the slow cooker on low, put the lid askew, and cook for about 10 hours or until the plum butter has reached the desired thickness. Keep in mind, the butter will thicken a tiny bit more as it cools.

4. Add the vanilla, stirring well to infuse the entire batch with its deliciousness. Adding the vanilla earlier in the process will cause

the vanilla to dissipate as the plums cook down. It's much better when you add it at the end.

5. Ladle the plum butter into pint jars.

6. Process in a hot water bath canner for 10 minutes, adjusting for altitude.

Raspberry Jalapeño Jam

In my mind, there aren't many flavors better than sweet and spicy at the same time. This makes the juxtaposition of raspberries and jalapeños a match made in sweet-spicy heaven.

Every year at Christmas, I dump this recipe out over a block of cream cheese and serve it with crackers. I could honestly just eat that and nothing else, although people seem to frown on guests that don't eat some of the turkey.

This jam makes a lovely and elegant appetizer, a tasty glaze for chicken or fish, and a delightful condiment on a turkey and Swiss cheese sandwich.

Makes approximately 7 (1-pint) jars

8 cups raspberries

4 cups sugar, divided

2 to 4 jalapeño peppers

¼ cup lemon juice

1. Prep the raspberries by washing them gently. Roughly puree in the food processor.

2. In a large bowl, layer the raspberry puree with 2 cups of sugar. Leave this in the refrigerator overnight. The next morning, there won't be very much juice. You most likely will not have enough to make syrup.

3. Carefully prep your jalapeños by wearing gloves, mask, and hazmat suit. (Okay, not really, but be careful 'cause those suckers can really make you burn if you touch your face after playing with them.) I use the food processor to get teeny tiny bits of jalapeño without massive pain and pepper juice exposure.

4. Stir raspberries, peppers, and lemon juice together in a large pot, bringing the mixture to a simmer.

5. Gradually stir in the remaining sugar and allow it to simmer until it reaches the desired texture.

6. Ladle the jam into your ready-and-waiting sanitized jars. Process in a water bath canner for 10 minutes, adjusting for altitude.

VARIATION: You can pair jalapeños with many different fruits. I've successfully married hot peppers with blackberries and peaches, and the results have been delicious.

Brown Sugar Peach Preserves

This is another holiday favorite at our house. I use half-pint jars, which contain the perfect amount to pour over cream cheese, yogurt cheese, or baked Brie. This sophisticated appetizer is best served with simple, hearty crackers. Trust me; you'll look fancy when you serve it!

For a variation on the recipe, you can add jalapeños for some sweet and spicy goodness. To make both recipes at once, ladle out your Brown Sugar Peach Preserves into one set of jars and then add jalapeños to the remaining jam for two flavors in one batch: Brown Sugar Peach Preserves and Sweet and Spicy Pepper Peach Jam. Keep the seeds in your jalapeños for a spicier flavor.

Makes approximately 7 (1-pint) jars

7 pounds fresh peaches

2 cups white or turbinado sugar

¼ cup lemon juice

2 cups brown or muscovado sugar

¼ cup finely chopped jalapeño peppers (optional)

1. Prep your fruit by washing it carefully. If the peaches are not organic, make a baking soda rinse (see page 13) to help remove the pesticides.

2. Smush your fruit. For this particular jam, I like to puree most of the fruit (including the skins) and then finely chop a few for added texture.

3. Layer the peaches and the white or turbinado sugar in a large crock and leave it in the refrigerator overnight.

4. The next day, drain the peaches using a fabric-lined colander over a large bowl for at least 2 hours.

5. In a stockpot, stir the peach puree, peach chunks, and lemon juice together well.

6. Bring the mixture to a boil over medium heat, stirring frequently.

7. Once mixture is boiling, stir in the brown or muscovado sugar and the jalapeños, if using, then reduce to a simmer. Be sure to stir frequently until it reaches the desired consistency.

8. Ladle the jam carefully into your awaiting sanitized jars, wipe the rims, and cap your jars with lids and rings.

9. Process in a water bath canner for 10 minutes and make adjustments for your altitude.

Spiced Fig Merlot Jam

This is another jam that looks super-fancy. Fresh figs are such a fantastic texture that they are basically in jam consistency as soon as you smush them. You can substitute any other red wine for the Merlot.

Makes approximately 8 (1-pint) jars

8 pounds fresh figs	1 tablespoon ground cinnamon
2 cups lemon juice	½ teaspoon ground cloves
3 cups sugar	1 cup of Merlot

1. Wash figs and remove stems.

2. Roughly puree figs in the blender or food processor.

3. In a stockpot, stir in all ingredients except the wine, and bring to a boil.

4. Once mixture is boiling, add the wine and reduce to a simmer until the jam is the consistency you desire.

5. Ladle the hot jam into sanitized jars.

6. Process the jars for 13 minutes, adjusting for altitude.

Rockin' Rhubarb and Strawberry Jam

This is a wonderful seasonal combo. Strawberries and rhubarb ripen at about the same time, and they go together like peas and carrots.

Makes approximately 7 (1-pint) jars

2 pounds strawberries

1 ½ pounds rhubarb

3 to 4 cups of sugar, to taste

¼ cup lemon juice

1. Prep your fruit by washing it carefully. Remove the stems of the strawberries and roughly chop the rhubarb.

2. Smush your fruit. We like this jam better if it's a little bit chunky, so don't go crazy unless you truly hate chunky jam.

3. Layer the fruit and 3 cups of sugar in a large crock and leave it overnight in the refrigerator.

4. The next day, drain the concoction using a fabric-lined colander over a large bowl for at least 2 hours.

5. In a stockpot, stir your fruit mixture and lemon juice together well.

6. Bring the mixture to a boil over medium heat, stirring frequently.

7. Once the jam is boiling, taste test it, taking care not to burn a layer of skin off your tongue. Stir in the extra sugar if necessary. Reduce to a simmer. Stir frequently until the jam reaches the desired consistency.

8. Ladle the jam carefully into your awaiting sanitized jars, wipe the rims, and cap your jars with lids and rings.

9. Process in a water bath canner for 10 minutes and make adjustments for your altitude.

12 WAYS TO USE HOMEMADE JAM THAT DON'T INVOLVE TOAST

If you're anything like me, sometimes you can go a teeny little bit…well… overboard…with the jam making. And by overboard, I mean that at the end of summer you have to resort to stashing jars under your bed and in the cabinet beneath the television to make room for them all.

Since there's only so much toast that one family can consume, here are some other delicious ways to use your jam.

1. **Top your yogurt with it.** You know those icky, artificially flavored fruit-bottom yogurts you can get at the store? Well, you make your own version of these by adding a hefty spoonful of peach jam to some vanilla-flavored yogurt. I always make my own yogurt, so this is a nice scratch meal from start to finish. You can even enthusiastically stir it into the yogurt to come up with a deliciously sweet, fruity yogurt.

2. **Serve it with cheese and crackers.** If you want to look fancy, set up a cheese plate with a tart-flavored jam in the middle. Top a cracker with a slice of cheese and a teeny dollop of jam. I like peach, blackberry, and Raspberry Jalapeño (page 52) for this. If you serve wine along with this dish, people will think they've stumbled into cocktail hour at the Waldorf Astoria.

3. **Turn it into a pancake topping.** Thin your blueberry jam with a little bit of fruit juice. I like grape juice because it is mild and absorbs the flavor of the jam. Warm the mixture in a saucepan, ladle over pancakes or waffles, and top with whipped cream. Serve immediately.

4. **Add it to smoothies.** Just a couple of tablespoons of jam will add a new twist to your favorite smoothies. Strawberry jam in a chocolate protein smoothie is a favorite in our house.

5. **Make a marinade with it.** Using a food processor, mix peach preserves (or pepper peach preserves, if you like it spicy), soy sauce, garlic, and a dash of orange juice. Place in a large zip-top

bag to marinate pork or chicken before grilling. Make some extra marinade for basting.

6. **Make jam-filled muffins**. Line a muffin tin with muffin cups. Fill each cup halfway with batter. Add a tablespoon of blackberry jam, then fill the cup to the top with batter. Bake as usual. The jam will be ridiculously, blazingly hot when fresh out of the oven, so don't eat these until they have thoroughly cooled.

7. **Make thumbprint cookies**. Make your favorite shortbread batter and place cookie-sized amounts on a baking sheet. Press your thumb into the raw cookie, then fill the indentation with your fanciest jam. We use Spiced Fig Merlot Jam (page 54) or Blueberry Lemon Jam (page 47) for this. Bake as usual.

8. **Crepe filling**: Using a food processor, mix ¼ cup of Rockin' Rhubarb and Strawberry Jam (page 55) with 8 ounces of cream cheese and process it until it's fluffy. Add this filling to crepes. To serve, drizzle a little of the pancake topping on them, add some slivered almonds, and top with a dollop of whipped cream.

9. **Have an ice cream social**. Using a fork, stir some red grape juice into strawberry or raspberry jam until it reaches the desired consistency. Top your ice cream with this for sundaes.

10. **Make a fancy baked Brie**. This is another yummy holiday recipe. Roll out some pastry; you can make your own or use refrigerated crescent roll dough. Add a peeled wheel of Brie to the center. Top the Brie with your favorite jam—Spiced Fig Merlot (page 54) or blackberry work beautifully for this. Pull the pastry up over the top and pinch it together. Bake according to the directions on the pastry dough, or according to your recipe. Check the dough to be sure it's done—you may need to bake it a bit longer, and if it is becoming overly brown, cover the top lightly with a sheet of tinfoil. Allow this to sit at room temperature for half an hour before serving. Slice into triangles and enjoy the gooey goodness.

11. **Add it as a layer in a cake**. When making a layer cake, add a layer of jam in the center instead of frosting. Try blueberry jam in a lemon layer cake for a delicious taste sensation.

12. **Dehydrate into fruit leather**. I do this at the end of summer when I need to free up some jars for the year's harvest. If you have a dehydrator, line your dehydrator sheets with parchment. Spread your jam onto the sheets in an even layer. Place in the dehydrator on low or at 135°F. Check it after 6 hours. Depending on the humidity in your area, it will take anywhere from 6 to 12 hours to dehydrate. Slice it while it's still warm, then allow it to cool before putting it away. (I have tried making fruit leather in the oven but have never had satisfactory results, although lots of folks on the internet claim to have the magic touch, if you want to try it out!)

There you go! Jam: it's not just for biscuits and toast anymore!

CHAPTER 6

Getting Condimental

Sassy Salsa Fresca

This recipe can be made more mild by reducing the amount of jalapeños, or more spicy by keeping all of the seeds from the peppers. If you *hate* cilantro, you can use parsley instead. You can use a food processor to make this recipe quicker or you can hand chop every single bit of it—it's all up to your personal combination of time and laziness.

Makes approximately 6 (1-quart) jars

8 pounds prepped tomatoes (see tomato prep, page 38)

4 cups seeded, chopped bell peppers

½ cup chopped jalapeño peppers, white pith removed

5 cups chopped onion

4 cloves garlic

4 to 6 tablespoons fresh cilantro or parsley leaves

1½ cups lemon or lime juice

1 teaspoon chili powder

1 (6-ounce) can tomato paste (optional)

1. Using your food processor, add the tomatoes, peppers, onion, garlic, and cilantro or parsley. Process on the "chop" function until you've reached the desired chunkiness.

2. Place a cotton towel in a colander over a large bowl or pot, then pour the chopped veggies in. Allow mixture to drain overnight in the refrigerator.

3. Once your veggies have adequately drained, add them into a large bowl or stockpot, then stir in your lemon or lime juice, chili powder, and tomato paste, if you're using it.

4. Ladle the salsa into the prepared jars.

5. Wipe the lip of the jars, place the lids and rings on them, and place them in the water bath canner.

6. Process for 15 minutes, adjusting for altitude.

"It's Easy Being Green" Tomato Salsa

This can be mixed with a basic white sauce to create the best enchilada sauce on the planet! Note that this salsa has a little more liquid than other types.

Makes approximately 8 (1-pint) jars

7 cups prepped green tomatoes (see tomato prep, page 38)

3 jalapeño peppers

1 green bell pepper

2 large onions

3 cloves garlic

½ cup cilantro

2 teaspoons ground cumin

1 teaspoon salt

½ cup lime juice

1. Using a food processor, chop tomatoes, peppers, onions, and garlic until they reach the desired chunkiness.

2. Pour the processed veggies into a large stockpot. Stir in cilantro, cumin, salt, and lime juice.

3. Bring to a boil, then reduce heat and simmer for 5 minutes.

4. Ladle green salsa into your ready-and-waiting pint jars, leaving a ½ inch of headspace at the top.

5. Process the jars in a water bath canner for 20 minutes, adjusting for altitude.

Peachy-Keen Salsa

This sweet-and-spicy salsa is mouth-watering over rice, chicken, pork, or fish. Pop a bow on this pretty little jar of peachy goodness for a lovely and elegant homemade gift.

Makes approximately 8 (1-pint) jars

INGREDIENTS

8 cups chopped, peeled peaches

1 large red onion, finely chopped

4 to 6 jalapeño peppers, seeded and finely chopped

1 red bell pepper, diced

6 cloves garlic, finely minced

½ cup cilantro

1 tablespoon ground cumin

½ cup apple cider vinegar

1 cup sugar

1. In a large stockpot, combine all ingredients except sugar. Mix well and bring to a boil.

2. Reduce heat. Stir in the sugar and return to a boil for 1 minute.

3. Ladle the salsa into your prepared jars.

4. Process in a water bath canner for 15 minutes, adjusting for altitude.

The Real Tomato Ketchup

Once you try this taste-of-summer condiment, those little packets and squirt bottles will never satisfy your ketchup craving again. This is a big project but it will keep you, and possibly your neighbors and friends, in the red stuff for a year. Using your blender will definitely speed things along. Use Roma, Sam Marzano, plum, or other paste tomatoes for this recipe.

Makes approximately 9 (1-pint) jars

12 pounds prepped paste tomatoes (see tomato prep, page 38)

1 pound quartered onions

½ pound green bell peppers, sliced into strips

½ pound red bell peppers, sliced into strips

4½ cups apple cider vinegar

1 cup brown sugar

2 tablespoons canning salt

1 tablespoon dry mustard

½ tablespoon crushed chili peppers

¼ teaspoon ground allspice

½ tablespoon ground cloves

¼ teaspoon ground cinnamon

1. In batches, puree your tomatoes, peppers, and onions. Pour each pureed batch into a large stockpot.

2. Bring the mixture to a boil, then reduce heat and simmer for 1 hour, uncovered.

3. Stir in the vinegar and spices and then pour the entire mixture into your slow cooker. You are going to cook this on low heat for about 12 hours, uncovered. My slow cooker is oval, so I always put the lid on sideways to retain a bit of the heat while allowing the steam to escape.

4. Once the ketchup is at your preferred consistency, give it a taste and adjust the seasonings if necessary. When it's perfect, ladle it into pint jars.

5. Lid the jars and process them in a water bath for 15 minutes, adjusting for altitude.

Renegade Taco Sauce

I invented this sauce when a raccoon did a night raid on my tomato patch. The Renegade Raccoon took a single bite out of each of my newly ripe tomatoes and knocked some green ones to the ground. This sauce was my effort to salvage what was left, and it was so good that it has become a regular item in my pantry. (I decided that Raccoon Taco Sauce might bring up some unsavory mental images and named it Renegade Taco Sauce instead.)

That is a long way of saying that you can include up to 1 pound of green tomatoes without changing the product. You can also use half a cup of your own (very well drained) tomato puree instead of tomato paste—and by "very well drained," I mean drained for about two or three days.

Makes approximately 6 (1-pint) jars

5 pounds prepped tomatoes (see tomato prep, page 38)

1 large bell pepper

2 to 6 jalapeño peppers

3 cloves garlic

¼ cup cilantro leaves

1 large onion

½ cup white vinegar

1 can tomato paste

3 tablespoons chili powder

1 tablespoon ground cumin

1 teaspoon salt

1. Use your food processor and puree the tomatoes, peppers, garlic, cilantro leaves, and onions.

2. Pour the puree into a stockpot and stir in the remaining ingredients.

3. Bring the sauce to a boil and then reduce the heat. Simmer for 10 minutes, stirring frequently.

4. Taste time! Check to see if the spices need adjustment.

5. Ladle the hot sauce into pint jars.

6. Process the jars in a hot water bath for 20 minutes, adjusting for altitude.

Honey Vidalia BBQ Sauce

Your barbecues will never be the same after you make this sauce. People will clamor for a jar to take home, so you might want to consider making a double batch and doling the extras out for Christmas! This is a pressure canning recipe. Other sweet onions can be swapped out for the Vidalias.

Makes approximately 9 (1-pint) jars

12 pounds prepped Roma tomatoes (see tomato prep, page 38)

2 cups chopped Vidalia onion

2 cups chopped red bell pepper

6 cloves garlic, crushed

1½ cups honey

1½ cups apple cider vinegar	1 tablespoon canning salt
1 tablespoon dry mustard	1 teaspoon black pepper
1 tablespoon smoked Hungarian paprika	1 teaspoon cayenne pepper

1. Using a blender or food processor, puree tomatoes, onions, peppers, and garlic.

2. Pour the puree into a large stockpot and stir in all other ingredients.

3. Bring to a boil until honey is well absorbed, then pour the mixture into your slow cooker.

4. Taste test to see if your seasonings need any adjustment.

5. With the lid on sideways or askew so steam can escape, let sauce reduce for about 4 to 6 hours, stirring every once in a while. Check your consistency and keep in mind it will thicken a little more as it cools.

6. Ladle the sauce into your prepared jars, leaving ½ inch of headspace.

7. Process in a pressure canner for 25 minutes at 10 PSI, adjusting for altitude.

Cha-Cha Chili Sauce

This complex sauce, based on one my Granny used to make, is sweet, spicy, and tangy all at once. It's a delightful topping for all things savory and especially nice when the cold sauce contrasts against a hot food. All good Southerners know that pinto beans are not pinto beans without a little bit of chili sauce on top!

Makes approximately 8 (1-pint) jars

10 cups prepped ripe tomatoes	2 jalapeño peppers, finely diced
2 cups chopped white onions	1½ cups brown sugar
2 cups chopped green bell peppers	2 cups apple cider vinegar
2 cups chopped, peeled plums	5 teaspoons salt

1 teaspoon ground cinnamon

1 teaspoon dry mustard

2 tablespoons pickling spices, in a spice bag

1. Coarsely chop the tomatoes, reserving juice.

2. Combine all ingredients in a slow cooker and cook on low for 4 to 6 hours, with the lid askew to allow steam to escape.

3. Once the sauce has reached the desired consistency, remove spice bag and ladle sauce into pint jars.

4. Lid your jars and process in a water bath canner for 15 minutes, adjusting for altitude.

Asian Plum Sauce

You can only eat so much plum jam and plum butter, but if you're lucky enough to have a plum tree, you probably still have plums to spare. A great use for these plums is this Asian Plum Sauce, which you can use as a dipping sauce or a stir-fry sauce. Add crushed chili peppers to make a spicy version of this sauce, or an extra cup of sugar to make the sauce super sweet. Keep in mind that the flavors will intensify as it sits on the shelf.

Makes approximately 6 (1-pint) jars

6 pounds plums

3 cups packed brown sugar

1 cup apple cider vinegar

1 medium onion

6 cloves garlic

1 tablespoon fresh ginger, minced

1 tablespoon salt

1 tablespoon dry mustard

1 teaspoon crushed chili peppers (optional)

1 cup brown sugar (optional)

1. Wash plums well, then remove the pit. Puree them roughly in a food processor or blender, leaving the skins on.

2. In a stockpot, combine all ingredients except the additional cup of sugar, if using.

3. Simmer the mixture for 2 to 3 hours. The consistency will be thick and slightly sticky.

4. Do a taste test. If you want a sweeter plum sauce, add the remaining sugar and simmer until it is thoroughly incorporated.

5. When you are happy with the taste and texture, go ahead and fill your jars, leaving a ½ inch of headspace.

6. Lid your jars and process in a water bath canner for 15 minutes, adjusting for altitude.

Heatwave Sweet and Spicy Hot Sauce

This recipe provides a great way to use up those random hot peppers. Serrano, Anaheim, jalapeño—they all work well in this recipe. In our garden, we tend to have several different types growing. We put all of them into this sweet and spicy conglomeration that can be drizzled on just about anything to make it hotter and just plain better. But you've been warned: it's pretty darned hot!

Makes approximately 4 (1-pint) jars

3 pounds hot peppers, chopped with seeds in

8 cloves garlic, smashed

2 medium onions, chopped

2 pounds prepped tomatoes (see page 38)

3 cups apple cider vinegar

½ cup of sugar

2½ cups water

1. Add all of the ingredients to a large stockpot and bring it to a boil for 20 minutes, or until the vegetables are tender.

2. Use a blender or food processor to puree the mixture.

3. Add the puree to sanitized pint jars, leaving ½ inch of headspace.

4. Wipe the rims of the jars, put the lids on, and then process them in a water bath canner for 10 minutes, adjusting for altitude.

CHAPTER 7

In a Pickle

Pickles are that marvelous and delicious exception to the rule stating that vegetables must be processed in a pressure canner. Because of the acid used in the pickling process, pickles may be water bath canned.

You must always use a vinegar that is a distillation of at least 5 percent. This won't be difficult; nearly all vinegars, even the cheapest brands, are distilled to that percentage. However, be sure to check, because if you use a vinegar with a lower acidity, you could be putting your family at risk for… wait for it…botulism.

Note that different jar sizes are recommended for different recipes. Relishes are often jarred in half-pint jars to prevent contamination after opening. Larger items, such as pickles, are often canned in larger jars.

A Dilly of a Relish

This recipe can be made with the overabundance of zucchini or cucumbers that you probably have, or even a combination of the two. However, for the purposes of this recipe, we'll just be discussing cucumbers. You can use whatever type of onion you'd like for this relish, but red onions add a lovely color.

Makes approximately 8 (½-pint) jars

6 pounds finely chopped pickling cucumbers

½ cup canning salt

2 teaspoons ground turmeric

3 cups water

2 large onions, finely chopped

4 cloves garlic, finely minced

⅓ cup white sugar

2 tablespoons dill seeds

3 cups white vinegar

1. Place chopped cucumbers in a glass bowl, sprinkle with salt and turmeric, and cover with water for 2 hours. This will help to draw the liquid out of your cukes (or zukes) so that your relish isn't runny.

2. Drain cucumbers and rinse under cold water in a colander, squeezing out the excess water with your hands.

3. Combine cucumbers, onions, garlic, sugar, dill seeds, and vinegar in a saucepan and bring to a boil.

4. Reduce heat and simmer 10 minutes.

5. Ladle into jars leaving ½ inch of headspace.

6. Process in a water bath canner for 15 minutes, adjusting for altitude.

Holy Jalapeño Relish

Jalapeño relish is probably the most requested out of all of my home-canned goodies, so much so that I planted a full dozen jalapeño plants in the garden to supply myself with the necessary veggies.

Use this to add more heat on anything you'd like to be spicier. It's great on chili, tacos, sausages, and more! This relish gets a workout at our house because some family members like spicy food and some do not, so we can customize the heat to suit ourselves.

Most of the heat is in the seeds. Use or do not use the seeds accordingly to turn up (or down) the heat in your finished product. If you want a condiment with less heat, replace up to half of the jalapeños with green bell peppers.

Makes approximately 8 (½-pint) jars

5 pounds finely chopped jalapeño peppers

2 cups sugar

4 cups white vinegar

½ cup cilantro leaves (optional)

1. In a food processor, finely chop the peppers. Don't turn them into a pureed mush; make them the consistency of a relish.

2. In a large pot, stir the sugar into the vinegar and bring to a boil. Immediately turn off the heat once boil is achieved.

3. Use your food processor to chop the cilantro leaves, if you are using them, then stir them into your chopped peppers.

4. Ladle the uncooked peppers and cilantro into your canning jars, then spoon the liquid over the mixture, allowing ½ inch of headspace.

5. Process the jars in a water bath canner for 10 minutes, adjusting for altitude.

Southern Belle Kitchen Sink Chow-Chow

The beauty of this recipe is in the fine art of making something delicious out of something that you have running out your ears. You can make this with any combination that suits your overflow situation at the time—zucchini, green tomatoes, cabbage, summer squash, cauliflower, or whatever else you've got. You can use brown or white sugar for this recipe, too; both result in an equally delicious concoction.

Chow-chow is generally served in the South as a condiment for pinto beans or field peas alongside a chunk of cornbread. However, it lends a sweet and spicy crunch to any simple fare.

Makes approximately 6 (1-pint) jars

8 cups chopped assorted veggies	2 whole allspice berries
1 cup finely chopped onion	3 whole cloves
1 cup diced red bell pepper	2 cups apple cider vinegar
¼ cup finely minced jalapeño pepper	2 cups sugar
2 teaspoons celery seeds	2 teaspoon dry mustard
2 teaspoons whole white mustard seeds	1 teaspoon ground turmeric
	1 teaspoon ground ginger
2 teaspoons coriander seeds	

1. Place all veggies in a colander over a bowl and sprinkle them with salt. Leave this in the fridge overnight to remove extra moisture.

2. Fill spice bag with celery seeds, mustard seeds, coriander, allspice, and cloves.

3. Mix the remaining ingredients in a large, non-reactive stockpot to create a brine. Add spice bag to brine.

4. Bring brine to a boil then drop it to a simmer for 10 minutes, stirring often to dissolve the sugar.

5. Stir in the veggies and heat through for about 5 minutes, or until warm.

6. Ladle this mixture into jars no larger than 1 pint, leaving ½ inch of headspace.

7. Lid the jars and process in a water bath canner for 10 minutes, adjusting for altitude.

Sweet-as-Can-Be Relish

Brighten up your burgers with this sweet and simple cucumber relish. Once you taste the freshness of your own relish, you will never eat the artificially colored and high-fructose corn syrup–laden grocery store relish again!

Makes approximately 6 (½-pint) jars

4 pounds finely chopped pickling cucumbers

½ cup canning salt

½ cup white vinegar

2⅓ cups sugar

4 tablespoons mustard seeds

3 cloves garlic, finely minced

2 tablespoons celery seeds

2 cups diced red bell pepper

2 cups finely chopped white onion

1. Place cucumbers in a large glass bowl and stir in the salt. Allow them to sit on the counter at room temperature for 4 hours.

2. Drain cucumbers and rinse in a colander under cold water, squeezing out the excess water with your hands.

3. Combine garlic, sugar, mustard seeds, celery seeds, and white vinegar in a saucepan and bring to a boil.

4. Reduce heat and stir in cucumbers, onions, and peppers, then return to a full boil.

5. Reduce heat and simmer the mixture for 10 minutes.

6. Ladle the hot relish into pint or half-pint jars, allowing ½ inch of headspace.

7. Lid the jars and process in a hot water bath canner for 10 minutes, adjusting for altitude.

British Branston Pickle

CC, my bestie from the UK, introduced me to this deliciousness. This sweet and sour condiment makes excellent use of random bits of garden produce. It is especially complimentary to dishes made with cheddar or blue cheese.

Makes approximately 5 (½-pint) jars

4 cups (about 20 ounces) chopped, peeled rutabaga

1 head cauliflower

3 carrots

2 onions

2 small zucchinis

2 Granny Smith apples, peeled and cored

1 cup chopped dates

12 gherkin pickles, diced

5 cloves garlic, minced

1 cup packed brown sugar

2⅔ cups malt vinegar

2½ cups water

⅓ cup lemon juice

¼ cup Worcestershire sauce

2 teaspoons salt

2 teaspoons mustard seeds

1½ teaspoons ground allspice

¼ teaspoon cayenne pepper

1. Using a food processor, finely chop the first 9 ingredients in batches.

2. Pour the veggies into a large saucepan and stir in remaining ingredients.

3. Bring the mixture to a boil, then pour into a slow cooker. Keeping lid askew, cook on low for 4 to 6 hours until the sauce has reached the desired consistency.

4. Ladle into pint jars, allowing ½ inch of headspace.

5. Lid your jars and process a water bath canner for 15 minutes, adjusting for altitude.

Dill-icious Sour Garlic Pickles

Grape leaves or blackberry leaves are used for these pickles because the tannin helps keep the pickles crisp. If you don't have access to grape leaves, there are commercial stay-crisp additives on the market. However, I personally prefer the natural options whenever possible.

Makes approximately 8 (1-quart) jars

10 pounds cucumbers, 3 to 4 inches in length

2 tablespoons black peppercorns

2 tablespoons mustard seeds

2 tablespoons coriander seeds

2 tablespoons dill seeds

1 tablespoon allspice berries

12 bay leaves, crumbled

4 cups white vinegar

4 cups water

½ cup canning salt

1 grape leaf per jar

2 heads dill per jar

2 cloves crushed garlic per jar

a few flakes of crushed chili peppers per jar (optional)

1. Scrub your cucumbers with a vegetable brush, then soak them in an ice water bath for 2 to 6 hours.

2. Combine peppercorns, mustard, coriander seeds, dill seeds, allspice, and crumbled bay leaves in a small bowl. Mix well. This will serve as your spice mix.

3. Combine white vinegar, water, and canning salt in a stockpot and bring to a rolling boil for 5 minutes.

4. Place a grape leaf in the bottom of each jar. Then add to each jar approximately 6 to 8 cucumbers, a tablespoon of your spice mix, the fresh dill, and the garlic. You can process the cucumbers whole or cut them into spears, depending on your personal preference.

5. Pour the hot brine over the contents of each jar.

6. Lid your jars and process in a water bath canner for 10 minutes, adjusting for altitude.

7. Remove the jars from the canner *immediately* for a crisper pickle.

8. This is the hard part—wait 7 to 10 days before popping open a jar for best results.

I Like Bread and Buttah Pickles

You have to sing that song by the Newbeats when making these pickles—it's the rule!

Makes approximately 6 (1-quart) jars

5 to 7 pounds (4- to 6-inch) cucumbers, cut into ¼-inch slices

2 pounds white onion, thinly sliced into rings

½ cup canning salt

3 cups white vinegar

2 cups white sugar

2 tablespoons mustard seeds

2 teaspoons ground turmeric

2 teaspoons celery seeds

1 teaspoon ground ginger

1 teaspoon peppercorns

1 grape leaf per jar

1. Place cucumber and onion slices in a large glass bowl, layering with canning salt.

2. Cover the salted veggies with ice cubes and allow them to stand in the refrigerator for 2 hours.

3. Drain veggies in a colander, then rinse and drain again.

4. Combine all other ingredients except for grape leaves in a large saucepot; bring to a boil.

5. Pack your sanitized jars with one grape leaf in the bottom of each, if using. Top with the cucumbers and onions.

6. Pour the hot brine over the contents of your jars, leaving ½ inch of headspace.

7. Lid the jars and process in a water bath canner for 10 minutes, adjusting for altitude.

8. These pickles, like all pickles, get better with time. Wait for at least a week before opening them.

Southern-Style Sweet Pickles

These are the kind Granny used to make, if your Granny is a sweet little Southern old lady like mine was.

Makes approximately 7 (1-quart) jars

8 pounds (3- to 4-inch long) pickling cucumbers

⅓ cup canning salt

1 tablespoon black peppercorns

1 tablespoon mustard seeds

1 tablespoon coriander seeds

½ tablespoon allspice berries

4 whole cloves

3 bay leaves, crumbled	3½ cups white vinegar
2 teaspoons celery seeds	1 grape leaf, per jar
4½ cups white sugar	

1. Place scrubbed cucumbers in a large glass bowl, layering with canning salt.

2. Cover the salted veggies with ice cubes and allow them to stand in the refrigerator for 2 hours.

3. Drain veggies in a colander, then rinse and drain again.

4. Make pickling spice by thoroughly mixing peppercorns, mustard seeds, allspice berries, cloves, bay leaves, and celery seeds.

5. In a large saucepan, combine sugar and vinegar with 3 tablespoons of pickling spice and bring to a boil.

6. Cut off the hard ends of the cucumbers and pack them into jars on top of a grape leaf.

7. Pour hot syrup over the contents of the jars, leaving ½ inch of headspace.

8. Process in a hot water bath canner for 10 minutes, *immediately* removing the jars when the processing time is up.

Random Pickled Veggies

When you have too much produce left in your garden to eat right away but not enough to can any one thing at the end of the season, make yourself some Random Pickled Veggies to enjoy throughout the winter. The ingredients list is flexible; it's actually more of an ingredients *suggestion* list. Go with what you have, but just try to keep the total sum of veggies the same. You can make these spicy if you include hot peppers. If you don't have hot peppers, you can substitute crushed chili peppers.

Makes approximately 6 (1-quart) jars

1 pound zucchini, cut into ¼-inch slices	1 pound green or yellow beans, ends removed
	1 pound carrots, cut into ¼-inch coins

1 pound cauliflower, cut into large florets

½-pound baby pearl onions, peeled or 1 pound white onion, sliced

2 bell peppers, cut into strips

3 cups apple cider vinegar

2 cups brown sugar

2 tablespoons dry mustard

2 tablespoons mustard seeds

1½ tablespoons canning salt

1 teaspoon ground cinnamon

1 teaspoon ground ginger

hot peppers, sliced lengthwise (optional)

1. Combine all veggies in a large bowl and set aside.

2. Add remaining ingredients in a large saucepan and bring the mixture to a boil.

3. Immediately reduce heat, stir in the veggies, and return to a boil. Reduce heat and simmer for 15 minutes.

4. Pack veggies and liquid into pint jars, allowing ½ inch of headspace.

5. Lid the jars and process in a water bath canner for 15 minutes, adjusting for altitude.

Crazy Carrot Pickles

I passionately detest canned carrots, so I was seeking to preserve them in a way I might actually enjoy. After some tweaking and experimenting, I came up with these "crazy" carrot pickles.

Makes approximately 6 (1-quart) jars

6 pounds carrots, peeled and trimmed to fit your jars

4 cups water

4 cups apple cider vinegar

½ cup brown sugar

4 tablespoons canning salt

1 tablespoon dill seeds

½ tablespoon black peppercorns

6 cloves garlic, crushed

1. Cut your carrots into spears. The size of your jars will determine the size of your carrot pieces.

2. Combine water, vinegar, sugar, and salt in a saucepan and bring it to a boil.

3. Add the other spices evenly across your sanitized jars, then fill jars snugly with carrots.

4. Pour the brine over the contents of the jars, leaving a ½ inch of headspace.

5. Wipe the lip of the jar, put on the lid, and process the carrot pickles in a boiling water bath for 10 minutes, adjusting for altitude.

Pleasantly Pickled Red Onions

Pickled onions create a milder and sweeter flavor than you'd get by just topping a burger or sandwich with a slice of raw onion, and they're far more elegant. They are also a lovely addition to a salad; you hardly need dressing when you have these babies and a little of the liquid drizzled over your greens.

Makes approximately 8 (½-pint) jars

5 cups red onion, thinly sliced into rings

2 cups red wine vinegar

2 cloves garlic, smashed

1 whole clove

¼ cup brown sugar

1. Thinly slice red onion.

2. Cry.

3. Once you can see again, bring vinegar, garlic, clove, and brown sugar to a boil in a saucepan, then immediately reduce heat and simmer for 5 minutes.

4. Fish out the large pieces of garlic and discard.

5. Stir the onions into the pot and return to a boil, stirring constantly.

6. Reduce heat and simmer for about 5 minutes, until the onions are soft.

7. Ladle the onions into pint jars and disperse liquid evenly, allowing ½ inch of headspace.

8. Lid the jars and process them in a water bath canner for 10 minutes, adjusting for altitude.

A Peck of Pickled Peppers

These spicy pickled peppers are great for topping sandwiches, nachos, or even salads. Anything you want to jazz up with a little bit of "bite" will be made better with these pickled peppers. You can use any peppers you like; they can be any mixture of banana, jalapeño, bell, serrano, Anaheim, or any pepper that strikes your fancy or grows in your garden. Also, I'm not really sure how much a "peck" is, but it has a certain ring to it.

Makes approximately 8 (1-pint) jars

8 pounds peppers

1 cup water

5 cups white vinegar

1 cup white sugar

4 tablespoon canning salt

1 onion

4 cloves garlic, crushed

1. Use only fresh, firm peppers for this. Wash your peppers and slice them into rings.

2. Bring water, vinegar, sugar, and salt to boil in a saucepan.

3. Thinly slice your onion and distribute it evenly across your jars. Top this with crushed garlic, then pepper rings.

4. Ladle the hot brine over the veggies in the jars, leaving ½ inch of headspace.

5. Process for 10 minutes in a hot water bath canner, adjusting for altitude.

CHAPTER 8

Fruit Frenzy

Fruit is loaded with vitamins, including vitamin C. A lack of vitamin C for an extended period will cause the deficiency disease scurvy.

Scurvy starts out with symptoms of paleness, lethargy, and feelings of depression. If the deficiency is not corrected, the sufferer will begin bleeding from the gums and other mucous membranes. As it worsens, tooth loss, jaundice, neuropathy, and eventually death will occur.

Imagine the grocery store is no longer an option. Where are you going to get your important nutrients? You will need to have them preserved and waiting on your shelves. So when the fruit trees are groaning with their bounty, take a break from biting into those fresh, juicy peaches and store up some jars of sunshine for the winter.

Be sure to use the canning liquid from your fruit. You can make a snazzy and delicious mixed drink for grown-ups, use it as the basis of a smoothie, or let the kids sip it exactly how it is. You can be fancy and pour some sparkling water over ice, then spike it with some fruity syrup from your jars. In the summer, you can also make some very tasty popsicles from the liquid.

Here is a reference for fruit canning. These times are all based on the raw-pack method of canning fruit in quart jars.

FRUIT CANNING QUICK REFERENCE	
FRUIT	TIME AT SEA LEVEL
Apple slices	25 minutes
Apricots	35 minutes
Berries	25 minutes
Cherries	30 minutes
Figs	55 minutes Add 2 tablespoons lemon juice
Grapefruit	15 minutes
Grapes	25 minutes
Nectarines	35 minutes
Oranges	15 minutes
Peaches	35 minutes
Pears	30 minutes
Pineapple	25 minutes
Plums	30 minutes

If you are canning a combination of fruits, look up the times for each ingredient individually. Always go with the longest time to make certain that your food is canned safely.

Canning Fruit in a Simple Syrup

The most basic way to can fruit is in a simple syrup. If you don't have the time or ingredients to be fancy, just about any fruit can be preserved this way. Here are the basic instructions; on page 46, you can find a chart with the processing times for different fruits.

There are light, medium, and heavy syrups. The difference between each of these is the proportion of sugar to water. You might want to vary the type of syrup based on the sweetness and flavor of the fruit. You can add a dash of vanilla, cinnamon, or cloves to jazz things up.

These amounts are based on what you'd need for a 7-quart canner load. An optional ingredient is 2 tablespoons of lemon or lime juice per each jar.

LIGHT SYRUP	MEDIUM SYRUP	HEAVY SYRUP
9 cups of water	8 cups of water	7 cups of water
3 cups of sugar	4 cups of sugar	6 cups of sugar

1. For whichever type of syrup you decide to make, bring the ingredients to a boil in a large stockpot, stirring frequently to combine the sugar. Once the sugar is dissolved, turn off the heat.

2. Pack your jars with raw fruit that has been prepped based on its type.

3. Top each jar of fruit with 2 tablespoons of lemon juice, if you're using it.

4. Ladle the hot syrup over the fruit.

5. Wipe the rim of the jar, put the lids on, and process for the appropriate amount of time based on the chart on page 29, adjusting for altitude.

No-Sugar Canning

For those who are avoiding sugar, canning fruit in juice may be the best option. You can use apple juice, white grape juice, or purple grape juice. I like to use a juice that corresponds to the fruit I'm canning, so I use apple juice for apples, white grape juice for light colored fruits like peaches, pears, or nectarines, and purple grape juice for darker fruits, like plums or berries.

For a 7-quart canner load, you'll need approximately 12 cups of the juice of your choice. I always add 2 tablespoons of lemon or lime juice to each jar of fruit but this is optional for most fruits, except as noted on the chart below.

1. Bring your juice to a boil in a large stockpot, then immediately turn off the heat.

2. Pack your jars with raw fruit that has been prepped based on its type.

3. Top each jar of fruit with 2 tablespoons of lemon juice, if you're using it.

4. Ladle the hot juice over the fruit.

5. Wipe the rim of the jar, put the lids on, and process for the appropriate amount of time based on the chart below, adjusting for altitude.

"How 'Bout Those Apples" Applesauce

When life gives you apples, make applesauce!

This recipe is perfect as baby food because it has only two ingredients: apples and water. None of that nasty high-fructose corn syrup slop in *this* applesauce!

Because of my inherent laziness, I used the "blender method" of making applesauce. This is the easy method. Shoot me if I one day have to try the difficult method, because this required almost three hours of hands-on work. The blender method requires far less cooking time and does not require you to peel the apples; this helps keep the vitamin content high. If you are leaving the peel on, it is especially important to clean the fruit carefully (see page 13).

Makes approximately 14 (1-quart) jars

1 bushel (40 pounds) cleaned apples   water, as needed

1. Chop and core the apples.

2. In batches, use a blender or food processor to puree the apples, skins and all, with just enough water to allow the blender to work.

3. Pour the puree into a large stockpot. Cook the sauce only long enough to heat it up.

4. As soon as the applesauce is merrily bubbling away, it's hot enough to ladle into your prepared jars. Be sure to allow at least ½ inch of headspace.

5. Lid your jars and process in a water bath canner for 20 minutes, adjusting for altitude.

Spiced Applesauce

If you'd like a little more flavor in your applesauce, this will fit the bill. I can't even express how great your house will smell while this simmers on the stove. No sugar is needed for this batch of fragrant deliciousness.

Makes approximately 14 (1-quart) jars

1 bushel (40 pounds) apples	⅛ cup ground ginger
lemon juice, as needed	2 tablespoons ground allspice
½ cup ground cinnamon	1 tablespoon ground cloves

1. Prep your apples by cleaning them as per the instructions on page 13.

2. Core the apples and cut them into chunks.

3. Using your blender or food processor, puree your apple chunks in batches. Add enough lemon juice to each batch to allow it to puree.

4. Pour the puree into the stockpot. Stir in all of the spices and bring to a light simmer. You aren't cooking the applesauce; you are merely heating it to help the flavors meld.

5. Lean over the pot and *smellllllllllll* how fantastic that spiced applesauce smells. Do not skip this vital step, or your entire applesauce making process will be disrupted and the whole batch could fail based on this alone.

6. Pour the hot applesauce into your prepared jars. Clean off the lip of the jar and top it with a lid and a ring.

7. Process your applesauce in a hot water bath canner for 20 minutes, adjusting for altitude.

Cranberry Apple Slices

These treats simply beg and plead to be topped with a crisp crumb topping, baked, and then smothered in vanilla ice cream. Of course, you can also grab a spoon and dig right into the jar! Because of the tartness of the cranberries, I do add sugar; however, it's only two cups divided across 6 quarts.

Note: If a pile of pears happens to fall into your lap, they are equally delicious when preserved this way!

Makes approximately 6 (1-quart) jars

6 pounds apples, washed well

1 cup lemon juice

5 cups apple juice

2 cups brown sugar

3 cups cranberries

6 cinnamon sticks

6 cloves

1. Core and slice apples, dipping them immediately in lemon juice to prevent browning.

2. Bring apple juice and brown sugar to a boil.

3. Carefully pour apple slices and cranberries into boiling juice and simmer for 5 minutes.

4. Place 1 cinnamon stick and 1 clove into each quart jar, then ladle fruit mixture and liquids into jars.

5. Make sure there are no air pockets, lid the jars, and process in a water bath canner for 25 minutes, adjusting for altitude.

Spicy Apple Rings

This is another recipe from the Granny files. I used to eat these until my mom had to pry the jar out of my sweaty little hands. So delicious!

When it comes to choosing apples for this recipe, I find that firm, tart apples like Granny Smith, Winesap, or Arkansas Black work best. With regard to red food coloring, you can get a natural one instead of using an artificial one. Unless you like eating bugs (cochineal is a red food color made from beetles), look for a red food color made from beets or other vegetables.

Some folks take a shortcut and throw in a handful of those little cinnamon heart candies to impart the traditional red color and spicy sweet flavor. This recipe has no red-hot hearts, but if you want to add some, replace the spices and half of the sugar with red-hot hearts. Even when you make it from scratch, this certainly isn't health food, but it adds some nice old-fashioned flair to a holiday dinner table.

Makes approximately 14 (1-pint) jars

12 pounds apples	3 tablespoons whole cloves
1 cup lemon juice	3 tablespoons ground cinnamon
10 to 12 cups sugar	1 teaspoon ground allspice
6 cups water	1 cinnamon stick per jar
1 ½ cups cider vinegar	1 teaspoon red food coloring (optional)

1. Prep your apples by washing them well and peeling them.

2. To make rings, slice the apples into circles, cutting across the diameter. Then remove the core by using a shot glass to push out the center, or carefully cut around it with a knife.

3. Dip the apple rounds in lemon juice and set them aside.

4. Combine all of the other ingredients except for the cinnamon sticks in a large stockpot. If using the food coloring, add it to the stockpot.

5. Bring the syrup to a boil, then reduce the heat and simmer it for 5 minutes. Stir frequently to dissolve the sugar.

6. Stack your apple rings into your quart jars. Pop a cinnamon stick down the center of the rings.

7. Ladle your deliciously spicy syrup over the apples. If possible, divvy up your cloves and allspice across the jars, because it looks purty.

8. Wipe the rims of the jars, put the lids on, and process in a hot water bath for 15 minutes, adjusting for altitude.

Spiced Mulled Pears

To take a break from regular sliced pears, try this decadently spiced version. This looks elegant and difficult, but honestly, it couldn't be easier! If you don't have all of the spices listed here, just double up on the ones you do have. Remember, versatility is key when it comes to canning!

Makes approximately 6 (1-quart) jars

10 pounds very firm pears	6 star anise pods
4 cups red grape juice	6 cinnamon sticks
1 cup orange juice	12 whole cloves
2 tablespoons vanilla extract	12 black peppercorns
½ cup brown sugar	

1. Peel pears, then cut them into eighths, discarding the cores.

2. In a stockpot, bring the grape juice, orange juice, vanilla, and brown sugar to a boil.

3. In each prepared jar, place 1 anise pod, 1 cinnamon stick, 2 cloves, and 2 peppercorns.

4. Pack the jars with pear sections, leaving ½ inch of headspace.

5. Ladle the syrup over the pears and remove any air pockets.

6. Lid the jars and process in a water bath canner for 20 minutes, adjusting for altitude.

Merlot-Spiced Pears

This is the be-all and end-all canned pear recipe. Not only does it taste decadent, but the way your house smells when you make it will bring everyone to the kitchen just to inhale it. When choosing a wine, opt for a drier red than you would usually drink. White sugar can be used in place of the turbinado.

Makes approximately 6 (1-quart) jars

10 pounds very firm pears	1 cup water
2 bottles Merlot	2 tablespoons ground cinnamon

| 1 teaspoon ground cloves | 2 cups turbinado sugar |

1. Pour the wine and water into a saucepan and bring to a simmer on low heat.

2. Mix the spices and sugar in a bowl until well combined.

3. While the wine mixture is simmering, stir in the sugar mixture. Stir with a whisk until the mixture is dissolved in the wine. Simmer on low heat for 15 minutes.

4. While the wine syrup is simmering, pack sliced pears into 6 sanitized quart jars.

5. Ladle the hot wine syrup over the pears, leaving ½ inch of headspace.

6. Process in a water bath canner for 20 minutes, adjusting for altitude.

Plain and Simple Pear Sauce

Another great way to use an abundance of pears is to make pear sauce. Slightly sweeter than applesauce, it can be used in baking or substituted in any recipe in which you would normally use applesauce. I like to leave the skins on my pears since so many of the nutrients lurk there.

Note: Pear sauce sometimes separates during the canning process. Don't be alarmed—it won't affect the quality or the taste. Simply shake the jar well before serving. Pear sauce generally has a thinner consistency than applesauce, so use the smallest amount of water possible.

Makes approximately 6 (1-quart) jars

15 pounds pears

dash of vanilla extract (optional)

water, as needed

1. Wash the pears carefully using the method described on page 13. If the pears are not organic, this will help to remove the pesticides if they have been sprayed.

2. Remove the cores and any dark spots.

3. Using a blender or food processor, puree the pears on a high setting, adding a teeny splash of vanilla if you're using it and water as needed to assist the blending.

4. Pour pear mixture into sanitized jars.

5. Process in a water bath canner for 20 minutes, adjusting for altitude.

"Everything Is Peachy" Peach Slices

A bushel of peaches will give you 20 to 24 quarts of peach slices to enjoy over the long winter. They are like bites of sunshine. Select freestone peaches; this will make your life far easier, as they give up the pit without the vast effort required to remove the pit from clingstone peaches. Trust me on this one.

Peaches can be peeled just like tomatoes. Dip them in boiling water for about a minute, then dunk them in ice water, and the skin will almost get up and walk off by itself. (Okay, I confess, you'll have to help it a little.)

Makes 20 to 24 (1-quart) jars

1 bushel peeled peaches	8 cups water
1 cup lemon juice	4 cups sugar
12 cups white grape juice	

1. Cut peeled peaches in half, then slice them. Immediately dip slices in lemon juice and then place them in a bowl.

2. In a stockpot, bring white grape juice, sugar, and water to a boil.

3. Place your peach slices into quart jars, leaving ½ inch of headspace.

4. Dump your bowl of lemon juice into the hot syrup.

5. Ladle the syrup over your peaches, then put the lids on the jars.

6. Peaches can be processed either in a water bath canner for between 30 and 40 minutes *or* in a pressure canner for 10 minutes at 5 PSI, adjusting for altitude. I prefer the pressure canner because I feel more vitamins are preserved in the shorter cooking time.

Plum Easy Cinnamon-Spiced Plums

The easiest thing about this plum recipe is that there is virtually *no work,* unless you choose to slice the plums in half and remove the stone at the time of processing. You will end up with a mushier plum this way, but a thicker sauce. You can use either grape juice or apple juice for this recipe.

Makes approximately 7 (1-quart) jars

14 pounds small plums

7 cinnamon sticks

14 whole cloves

7 cups white grape or apple juice

7 cups water

3 cups sugar (optional)

1. Wash plums well, using the method described on page 13.

2. If you are slicing the plums, cut them in half and remove the stone. If you are preserving them whole, poke the plums at each end using a fork—otherwise, your plums will explode in your jars during processing.

3. Pack your jars with plums.

4. Add one cinnamon stick and a couple of cloves to each jar.

5. On the stove, bring your mixture of juice, water, and sugar, if using, to a boil.

6. Ladle the hot liquid over the raw-packed plums in quart jars. Lid the jars.

7. To process, you can either process for 25 minutes in a water bath canner, *or* process for 1 minute at 5 PSI in a pressure canner, adjusting for altitude.

Tutti-Frutti Mixed Jars

Warning: Once you've tried this homemade fruit cocktail, you'll never be able to choke down that nasty, syrupy stuff from the store again. Your family will insist that you make this every single year! The mint adds a hint of fresh summery flavor to every jar, but is entirely optional.

This is a wonderful recipe for using whatever you have on hand. The proportions don't matter; use whatever is cheap and abundant for you. For this reason, there are no measurements with this recipe; it will be different every time. Use apple juice or white grape juice.

SUGGESTED FRUITS
Mixture of apples, apricots, cherries (pitted), grapes, nectarines, peaches, pears, and plums

1 cup lemon juice

3 tablespoons sugar per quart jar (optional)

1 cup apple or white grape juice for every cup of water

fresh mint (optional)

1. Wash all fruit carefully.

2. Cut fruit into bite-sized pieces and dip the pieces in lemon juice, then place them into jars, evenly dispersing the different types of fruit across your batch.

3. If you are adding sugar, spoon it on top of the fruit in the jars.

4. Fill a stock pot with equal parts juice and water.

5. Bring mixture to a boil and then ladle it over the fruit in your ready-and-waiting sanitized quart jars.

6. Add a sprig of mint, if using, to each jar. Lid the jars and process in a water bath canner for 20 minutes, adjusting for altitude.

Very, Very Orange Cherries

This sweet, sunny recipe turns out better if you process it in a pressure canner, but alternate instructions are present for those who don't have one. The main issue is one of texture. The pressure-canned cherries are significantly more firm.

Also, if you don't have one, get a cherry pitter. For less than $10, this investment will literally save you hours!

Makes approximately 7 (1-quart) jars

10 pounds sweet cherries

3 cups red grape juice

3 cups orange juice

1 cup sugar

1. Using a cherry pitter, remove the pits from the cherries. Place cherries in quart jars.

2. In a stockpot, heat the juices and sugar until boiling.

3. Ladle the hot liquid into the jars, then run a rubber spatula around the inside of the jar to remove any air pockets.

4. Lid the jars and process them in a pressure canner for 10 minutes at 5 PSI, adjusting for altitude.

Note: If you do not have a pressure canner, add the cherries to the boiling juice and cook for 10 minutes before placing them in the jars. Then process them in a water bath canner for 20 minutes, adjusting for altitude.

Bring on the Berries

Berries are among the easiest fruits to can because they require practically *no* prep work, and are actually best when a raw-pack canning method is used.

This method works well with every berry that I have tried: blueberries, blackberries, raspberries, huckleberries, and strawberries have all been successful. You can also mix your berries for even more yumminess! Use whichever type of grape juice you prefer for this recipe.

Makes 1 quart jar

2 tablespoons lemon juice per quart jar

assorted berries, just under 2 pints per quart jar

2 tablespoons sugar per jar, optional

grape juice and water, in an equal ratio

1. Clean berries.

2. Place 2 tablespoons of lemon juice into each quart jar, then add in the berries, leaving ½ inch of headspace. Top with sugar if you're using it.

3. Bring your juice and water mixture to a boil in a large stockpot.

4. Ladle the liquid over the berries, lid the jars, then gently turn or shake them to remove air pockets from the bottom of the jar.

5. Berries can be processed either in a hot water bath canner for 20 minutes, *or* in a pressure canner for 10 minutes at 5 PSI, adjusting for your altitude.

CHAPTER 9

Venerable Vegetables

Ahh, vegetables. They are the reason I began gardening in the first place, and then from there, canning. My yearning for year-round, affordable, organic, non-GMO produce provided the jumping off point for my two favorite hobbies.

We eat lots of vegetables. I would be hard-pressed to afford them all at the natural food store. In the summer, the perfect solution is to raise my own veggies or hit up the farmer's market. But of course, we want vegetables in the winter too.

Taking it one step further, there may come a time when you must be self-sufficient and will only be able to eat what you can grow and preserve. Learning the best ways to store your garden bounty for the cold days ahead is vital.

Most of the vegetables listed here are canned simply with very little seasoning. It's not that we dislike flavor, but if there is less seasoning in the jar, you can cook them up however you want in the winter. This allows them to be used as ingredients in whatever meal you happen to be making and makes them far more versatile.

I use the raw-pack method whenever possible because, well... because I'm lazy. Running a close second to my laziness is that veggies that have been cooked and then canned are often too mushy. Canned veggies by their very nature are fairly mushy, and as an al dente veggie lover, it's a bit of an adjustment. If you don't like the textural result of some of your canning projects, be creative and think of other ways to use them. Try pureeing them and adding them to soup or mashed potatoes, for example.

If you are using salt, place the desired amount in the bottom of your sanitized canning jars. When you pour water over the contents, the salt will disperse. Our preference is ⅛ teaspoon in pint jars and ¼ teaspoon in quart jars. I recommend a non-iodized salt, like canning salt or sea salt, if you plan to add salt to your vegetables. Iodized salt can make the veggies turn ugly colors.

Note: Take advantage of the vitamins stored in the liquid by adding it to soup stock or using it for cooking grains like rice or barley.

Vegetables contain very little acid. Therefore, vegetables *must* be processed in a pressure canner. There is no gray area here, because the failure to do so can put you at risk for botulism (see more on page 11). A water bath canner does not reach and maintain a high enough temperature to kill off the bacteria that causes botulism, but a pressure canner does.

Here is a quick-reference chart for canning a wide variety of veggies.

Remember, vegetables are a low-acid food and must be processed in a pressure canner with a baseline of 11 PSI, and adjustments for altitude.

VEGETABLE CANNING QUICK REFERENCE		
FOOD	TIME FOR PINTS AT SEA LEVEL	TIME FOR QUARTS AT SEA LEVEL
Asparagus	30	40
Beans (green or yellow)	20	25
Beets	30	35
Carrots	25	30
Corn	55	85

VEGETABLE CANNING QUICK REFERENCE		
FOOD	TIME FOR PINTS AT SEA LEVEL	TIME FOR QUARTS AT SEA LEVEL
Lima Beans	40	50
Okra	25	40
Peas (field)	40	40
Peppers	35	not recommended
Potatoes (white)	35	40
Potatoes (sweet)	65	90
Pumpkin	55	90
Squash (winter)	55	90

Awesome Asparagus

We have found home-canned asparagus to be unpleasantly mushy on its own. With this warning in mind, if you end up with a windfall of asparagus, canned asparagus makes an ultra-delicious, tastes-of-springtime cream of asparagus soup.

Makes approximately 7 (1-quart) jars

15 pounds fresh asparagus

water as needed

salt (optional)

1. Wash your asparagus carefully and gently.

2. Cut the spears into the proper lengths to fit inside your jars, discarding the woody ends.

3. Set a large pot of water to boil.

4. If you are using salt, place the desired amount in the bottom of your sanitized canning jars.

5. Load up the jars with your asparagus spears, packing them in tightly.

6. Ladle or pour boiling water into the jars, allowing 1 inch of headspace.

7. Use a rubber spatula to remove any air pockets, then add more water if needed.

8. Lid the jars and process them in your pressure canner at 10 PSI for 30 minutes if using pint jars and 40 minutes if using quart jars. Remember to adjust for altitude.

Carrots with Honey

Carrots can be jarred in any of a wide variety of shapes: coins, spears, ruffles, large chunks, or even whole, if they fit in the jar! However, don't make them too small or they will be mushy and gross. This year I canned them whole, and they turned out with a far better texture than in previous years, when I cut them into various other shapes. The bigger the pieces are, the better the results are. A drizzle of honey in each jar intensifies the natural sweetness of the carrots.

Canned carrots work very nicely as an ingredient in baked goods.

Makes approximately 8 (1-pint) jars

10 pounds carrots

water, as needed

½ teaspoon honey or turbinado sugar per jar (optional)

salt (optional)

1. Wash your carrots, then peel and slice them as desired.

2. Set a large pot of water to boil.

3. If you are using salt, place the desired amount in the bottom of your sanitized canning jars. If you are using honey or sugar, add this to the bottom of the jars. Load up the jars with your carrot pieces, packing them in tightly.

4. Ladle or pour boiling water into the jars, allowing 1 inch of headspace.

5. Use a rubber spatula to remove any air pockets, then add more water if needed.

6. Lid the jars and process them in your pressure canner at 10 PSI for 25 minutes if using pint jars, or 30 minutes if you're using quart jars. Adjust for altitude.

A Cornucopia of Corn

If you are fortunate enough to hit the mother lode of fresh, non-GMO corn, don't hesitate to put it into jars for future consumption. There is quite honestly no comparison between freshly canned corn and the stuff you get from grocery store tin cans. For Southwestern flair, you can add some chopped peppers, onion, and a dash of chili powder to your corn.

Approximately three ears of corn will fill a pint jar when the kernels are removed from the cob. Corn expands in the pressure canner, so be sure you leave that inch of headspace!

3 ears makes 1 pint

corn on the cob

water, as needed

salt (optional)

1. Husk the corn and remove the silk with a vegetable brush. This is a messy, back-porch kind of job.

2. Start boiling a big pot of water.

3. Slice the corn off the cob as closely as possible. It will come off in strips.

4. Fill your jars with corn, leaving 1 inch of headspace.

5. Ladle boiling water into the jars, allowing 1 inch of headspace.

6. Use a rubber spatula to remove any air pockets, then add more water if needed.

7. Lid the jars and process them in your pressure canner for 55 minutes at 10 PSI, or 85 minutes if you're using quart jars.

Greenie Beanies

You can also use this process for wax beans or yellow beans, or (our favorite) a colorful combo of the three!

Makes approximately 7 (1-quart) jars

14 pounds green beans

water as needed

salt (optional)

1. Wash your beans carefully, then rinse them well.

2. Snap off the ends of your beans and then snap them into the desired size. Approximately 2-inch-long pieces fit very nicely in the jars.

3. Set a large pot of water to boil.

4. If you are using salt, place the desired amount in the bottom of your sanitized canning jars.

5. Load up the jars with your beans, packing them in tightly.

6. Ladle or pour boiling water into the jars, allowing 1 inch of headspace.

7. Use a rubber utensil to remove any air pockets, then add more water if needed.

8. Lid the jars and process them in your pressure canner at 10 PSI for 20 minutes if using pint jars, 25 minutes if using quart jars.

Peas Please

These instructions are for any type of field peas: green peas, purple hull peas, black-eyed peas, or crowder peas, for example. If you wish to can black-eyed peas with bacon, see the Hoppin' John recipe on page 122.

Makes approximately 9 (1-pint) jars

9 pounds peas

water, as needed

salt (optional)

1. Find a comfy place to sit with a couple of bowls, recruit some help, and start shelling peas.

2. Set a large pot of water to boil.

3. If you are using salt, place the desired amount in the bottom of your sanitized canning jars.

4. Load up the jars with your beans, packing them in tightly.

5. Ladle boiling water into the jars, allowing 1 inch of headspace.

6. Use a utensil to remove any air pockets, then add more water if needed.

7. Lid the jars and process them in your pressure canner at 10 PSI for 30 minutes if using pint jars, or 40 minutes if using quart jars.

Funky Chunky Squash or Pumpkin

It's common canning knowledge that you shouldn't can pumpkin and squash. However, it is actually just pumpkin and squash *purees* that should not be canned. This is because the purees are so thick that they don't heat evenly, leaving them open to the risk of botulism. It's perfectly fine to can your pumpkin or squash in chunks in a pressure canner, and then puree them when you need them.

I leave my pumpkin and squash totally without seasoning so that they can be used flexibly in either sweet or savory dishes. We always save the seeds for roasting.

1 pound squash makes 1 quart

uncooked pumpkin or winter squash

boiling water, as needed

1. Cut up your pumpkin or squash and remove the rind, seeds, and strings. Cut it into 1-inch chunks.

2. You can raw-pack your pumpkin or squash. Fill your quart jars with cubes, leaving 1 inch of headspace.

3. Fill the jar with hot water, keeping an inch of headspace.

4. Slide a rubber utensil around the sides of the jar to remove air pockets.

5. Lid the jars and process them in your pressure canner 11 PSI for 90 minutes, adjusting for altitude.

Sweet and Sassy Coleslaw

Sometimes canned veggies can be sort of bland and a bit of a drag. Not so with this Sweet and Sassy Coleslaw! It has all of the delicious flavor of the slaw you might slave over to fix for a family barbecue, but it sits there patiently on the shelf, awaiting its day on the picnic table. Using red peppers and red onion adds a nice bit of color to the recipe, though you can omit the peppers if you prefer. This recipe is high enough in acid content to safely use a water bath canner, for which instructions are given.

Makes approximately 8 (1-pint) jars

3 heads cabbage	3 cups white vinegar
3 carrots	1 cup water
2 bell peppers (optional)	2 cups sugar
3 small onions	1 tablespoon celery seeds
3 teaspoons canning salt	2 teaspoon dry mustard

1. Shred all of the vegetables in a food processor. Toss them with salt, then put the veggies in a colander to drain.

2. Let the veggies drain for an hour. Then, squeeze them with your hands to get out any remaining liquid.

3. Meanwhile, make your dressing by combining all remaining ingredients in a saucepan and bring mixture to a boil for a minute or two. Remove from heat.

4. In a large bowl, toss together your vegetables and warm dressing.

5. Place the slaw into jars, allowing a ½ inch of headspace.

6. Process in a boiling water bath for 15 minutes for quarts, 20 minutes for pints. Be sure to adjust for your altitude.

Serving Suggestion: At serving time, I like to add just a teeny bit of vegetable oil; we prefer sunflower or olive. This gives it more of a "dressed salad" flavor than a "pickled veggie" flavor. This is not the mayo-based coleslaw that a lot of folks think of, but the Southern sweet-and-sour type. However, if your family prefers a creamy slaw, you can drain the liquid at serving time and toss the slaw in a bit of mayo.

Totally Tomatoes

I like to can some of my tomatoes plainly and simply. This way they are a little more versatile and I can use them in any type of recipe with any type of seasoning.

Because tomatoes are actually a fruit, not a vegetable, they have a high enough acid content to safely use a water bath canner. Instructions for both water bath canning and pressure canning are given.

Makes approximately 7 (1-quart) jars

20 pounds tomatoes

2 tablespoons lemon juice per jar

water, as needed

1. Prep your tomatoes as per the instructions on page 38.

2. Place your peeled, cored tomatoes in sanitized quart jars. You can cut them up or leave them whole.

3. Add 2 tablespoons of lemon juice to each jar.

4. Fill the jars with boiling water, leaving ½ inch of headspace.

5. Use a rubber utensil to remove any air pockets; failure to do this could cause your jars not to seal.

6. Lid the jars.

7. If you're using a water bath canner, process the tomatoes for 45 minutes, adjusting for altitude. If you're using a pressure canner, process the tomatoes for 15 minutes at 6 PSI, adjusting for altitude.

¡Ole, Ole! Tomatoes and Peppers

This is a homemade version of the store-bought canned Mexican-flavored tomato and pepper goodness, Rotel. It can be added to cheese sauce to make a delicious queso, pureed as a base for chili, or drained and thrown into some taco meat on the stovetop. The sky's the limit!

Use whichever hot peppers you have on hand for this recipe. Lemon juice can be substituted for lime juice, but I like lime juice better.

Makes approximately 7 (1-quart) jars

12 pounds of tomatoes, peeled and cut into chunks

3 bell peppers, diced

1 large onion, diced

2 pounds diced hot peppers

1 cup white vinegar

¼ cup sugar

4 tablespoons chili powder

2 tablespoons canning salt

1 tablespoon lime juice per jar

1. Put all of the ingredients except for the lime juice into a large stockpot and stir to combine everything.

2. Bring the mixture to a simmer, and allow it to cook uncovered for 45 minutes to reduce the liquid and meld the delicious flavors.

3. Add a tablespoon of lime juice to each pint jar then ladle in the super-yummy mixture, leaving ½ inch of headspace.

4. Pop the lids on and then process this in a water bath canner for 15 minutes, adjusting for altitude.

Tomato-Tomahto Juice

Some say tomato, some say tomahto. This thin puree is as simple as running your tomatoes through the blender, and possibly adding some garlic, onions, and salt to them. It can be used as a base for soup, chili, spaghetti sauce, enchilada sauce, or any other application that requires crushed tomatoes. I like to can this because it's pretty neutral and can be used in so many different recipes throughout the year.

I didn't give measurements with this recipe because this simple sauce can be made from any amount of tomatoes that you happen to lay hands upon. It is also a great way to use up soft or overripe tomatoes quickly.

1½ pounds tomatoes makes approximately 1 quart jar

assorted peeled tomatoes

½ small onion per jar (optional)

1 clove garlic per jar (optional)

sea salt or canning salt, to taste (optional)

1 tablespoon lemon juice per jar (optional if pressure canning)

1. Peel tomatoes and place them directly into the bowl of your food processor or pitcher of your blender. Approximately 3 cups of unprocessed tomato will fill a quart jar. If you're using onions and garlic, add those to the food processor at the same time.

2. Use the pulse option on your processor until the mixture reaches your desired consistency.

3. Pour this into a quart jar.

4. Repeat until you have a canner load of sauce.

5. Add a dash of salt, if using, to each jar. If you are water bath canning, add 1 tablespoon of lemon juice to each jar. If you are pressure canning, the lemon juice is not necessary.

6. In a water bath canner, process your sauce for 40 minutes, *or* process using your pressure canner for 25 minutes at 10 PSI, adjusting for altitude.

Snowfall Spaghetti Sauce

The rule in our house is that you don't open the spaghetti sauce until the first snow. My little one always eagerly awaits the first flake and runs home to tell me, "We're having spaghetti! It's snowing!" The reason we wait to open the sauce is because it gets better when it sits for a few months. The depth of flavor combined with the freshness of the ingredients makes this a hit. Each year I make at least 24 jars—enough sauce for my family to enjoy spaghetti twice a month.

Homemade marinara sauce is a world away from the stuff you buy in the grocery store. It's loaded with vitamins and nutrients, and not tainted by BPA, additives, and high-fructose corn syrup.

Don't be put off by the hands-on time needed to make this. Consider that if you made 14 from-scratch spaghetti dinners, it would take you far more time than the six hours that these two batches of sauce took.

It takes approximately 1.5 pounds of tomatoes to make 1 quart jar of sauce. The following instructions are for a canner-load full of sauce, or 7 quarts. Keep in mind that different types of tomatoes will yield different amounts of sauce, so there will be some variation.

Note: When it's time to can the sauce, don't worry if the consistency is still a little bit watery. Over its time on the shelf, it will thicken a little bit. You can always opt to cook it down for a bit longer to get it closer to the thickness you desire. If at serving time it is still runnier than you prefer, simply stir in a small tin of tomato paste to thicken it.

Makes approximately 7 (1-quart) jars

20 pounds tomatoes	⅓ cup dried oregano
2 bell peppers	⅓ cup dried basil
2 large onions	1 tablespoon ground cloves
1 to 2 heads garlic	1 tablespoon paprika
⅓ cup sugar	⅔ cup extra virgin olive oil
2½ tablespoons sea salt	black pepper, to taste
2½ tablespoons dried thyme	

SAUCE DIRECTIONS

1. Clean and peel 20 pounds of tomatoes as per instructions on page 38.

2. Using a food processor or blender, puree bell peppers, onions, and garlic.

3. Add the prepped tomatoes and veggies to a large stockpot. Add seasonings and olive oil.

4. With the lid on, bring the sauce to a simmer for about an hour, stirring occasionally. Then, remove the lid, drop the heat and

simmer gently for 3 more hours. Removing the lid will allow the liquid to evaporate so that the sauce can cook down and thicken.

5. To can the sauce, ladle it into quart jars, allowing 1 inch of head space.

6. Wipe the lip of your jars with a cloth dipped in white vinegar and then place the lids on.

7. Process the sauce in your pressure canner for 25 minutes at 7 PSI, adjusting for altitude.

8. Allow the jars to sit undisturbed for 12 hours, or until cooled. Test the seals before putting them away.

Now you have many quarts of delicious, authentic Italian marinara sauce to serve at pasta dinners to come. You can use this to make spaghetti and meatballs, chicken parmesan, as the base of an Italian vegetable soup, or you can thicken it to use as a pizza sauce. See the variations starting on page 141 to turn your beautiful marinara into a complete meal.

Mangia bene! (Eat well!)

CHAPTER 10

The Meat of the Matter

The recipes in this chapter are geared towards preparing the meat ingredients of a meal, rather than preparing a complete meal. Having a supply of already prepared basic meats on hand can go a long way toward speeding up mealtimes throughout the year. Canning meat is a great way to take advantage of a good sale or a bulk purchase without having to worry about what will happen if your freezer malfunctions or if you have a power outage.

When you think about canned meat, you probably get the idea of those icky store-bought mystery chunks that you can purchase. Home-canned meat is miles away from that. It can be most closely compared to meat that has been put in the slow cooker to simmer on low all day. Moist, tasty, and so tender that it falls apart when you put a fork to it.

The other benefit to canning your meat is that not only will it be preserved no matter your electricity situation, but it will be immediately ready to eat. If you have a way to cook, you won't have to waste much fuel actually cooking the meat. And in the worst case scenario, if you can't warm it up, it's safe to eat right out of the jar.

In a disaster situation, having sufficient protein is extremely important. If you perform hard manual labor without adequate protein, your body will begin to catabolize your muscles to provide it with necessary nutrients. This will weaken you physically at a time when you need to be at your peak.

Meats *must* be canned using a pressure canner—remember our talks about botulism? Most meat can be raw-packed, because the heat of the canner will thoroughly cook the meat while it is processed.

ABOUT ROAST BEAST

I use the term "Roast Beast" to apply to any type of non-poultry roast that you might acquire: pork, beef, bison, venison, moose, you name it. When you hit the mother lode, whether it's a great sale, a successful hunt, or a side of beef that's just arrived, take some time to can it right away. Then you won't be subject to the whims of the electric grid, and a great meal is as close as popping the lid off of a jar.

MEAT-CANNING PREP

I like to plan for a full day of prep, canning, and clean up when I have an abundance of meat in my freezer. This allows me to make the backbone of dozens of meals.

When dealing with a large amount of raw meat, I make it easy for myself by cutting open a cardboard box and laying it out on my counter. Then I use one cookie sheet to hold the meat and place my cutting board in another cookie sheet. This way I don't have to clean up a bloody mess after preparing all that meat for canning. (I'm sure you know this, but be certain to put a few drops of bleach in the wash water afterward in order to kill bacteria left from the raw meat.) A few other meat-canning tips:

- Use wide-mouth jars for canning meat so that it isn't a wrestling match to get it out at serving time. When you pressure can the meat it becomes fork tender, so you want to be able to remove it from the jar with minimum hassle.

- Even if you like highly seasoned food, don't go too crazy adding seasonings before canning. The flavors will greatly intensify, so use a light hand.

- Take special care when cleaning the rims of the jars, because the fat content in meat can interfere with proper sealing if it gets between the jar and the lid. Try dipping a cloth or paper towel in white vinegar to break down any grease lingering on the lip of the jar.

- Never add thickeners like flour or cornstarch to your liquid. You won't end up with gravy; you'll end up with a nasty, gloppy mess. You can make gravy with the liquid at serving time.

- Slice the roasts into pieces that will fit into your jars. Obviously, if you aren't using wide-mouth jars, those pieces will need to be smaller.

- Some separation of the sauce ingredients and the fat from the meat is perfectly normal. You can either discard the fat or stir it back in, depending upon your preference and dietary requirements.

Raw-Packed Roast Beast

Because the amount of your bounty will vary from batch to batch, this recipe is per jar, and meat measurements are approximate. Use any type of non-poultry hunk of meat for this.

1 pound meat makes 1 quart jar

1 pound roast

1 clove garlic

2 small cooking onions, halved

salt and pepper, to taste

water, as needed

1. Place a hunk of roast in each quart jar, leaving 1½ inches of space for the additional ingredients.

2. Add garlic, onions, salt, and pepper to each jar.

3. Pour water into the jars over the meat and veggies. Using a rubber spatula, run it down the sides of the jars to remove any air pockets, then add more water if needed. Allow 1 inch of headspace.

4. Use a cloth with some vinegar on it to wipe the lip of the jars. Lid the jars.

5. Using your pressure canner, process the jars for 90 minutes at 10 PSI, adjusting for altitude.

Serving suggestion: When you are ready to serve your roast, use the canning liquid to make gravy.

Barbecue Canned Beast

You may not want to can your entire beast as a simple roast, so another great way to preserve your meat is in a homemade barbecue sauce. This sweet sauce is especially nice with game, as it softens the flavor that some people find offensive. It can be used either for a full roast or for ground meat.

The result can be removed from the jar, shredded with two forks, and mixed in with the sauce for a tender pulled pork (or pulled whatever).

Feel free to use canned or fresh tomatoes for the sauce. If you're adding hot sauce, Frank's Red Hot is a favorite.

Makes approximately 6 (1-quart) jars

6 pounds beast	water, if needed

INGREDIENTS FOR SAUCE

½ cup fresh bell pepper	½ cup apple cider vinegar
6 cloves garlic	1 teaspoon Worcestershire sauce
3 small cooking onions	1 tablespoon hot sauce (optional)
6 cups crushed tomatoes	¼ teaspoon ground cloves
1 cup brown sugar	1 tablespoon paprika
1 cup honey	

1. Using a food processor, puree peppers, garlic, and onion.

2. Mix the puree, along with all other ingredients for the sauce, in a saucepan and bring to a boil.

3. Proceed with canning as for regular roast beast (see page 149) but replace the water in the recipe with barbecue sauce. If your jars don't have quite enough barbecue sauce to fill up completely, you can top them off with more water.

Deep South BBQ

This Southern classic can be made with any inexpensive roast, like beef or pork. The smoky flavorful meat only gets better as it sits in the jar.

Note: Pint jars hold approximately 1 pound of cooked meat

Makes approximately 6 (1-pint) jars

5 to 6 pounds roast

1 bottle of beer

2 large onions, pureed

2 cups ketchup

¼ cup prepared yellow mustard

½ cup brown sugar

¼ cup apple cider vinegar

1 tablespoon garlic powder

1 teaspoon black pepper

1 tablespoon liquid smoke

½ tablespoon Louisiana-style hot sauce

1. Place the roast and onions in a slow cooker, then pour a bottle of beer over them.

2. Cook on low for 10 hours. The meat should be so delightfully tender that it falls apart when you touch it with a fork.

3. Shred the meat with two forks, and return it to the cooking liquid in the slow cooker. Stir to combine.

4. In a saucepan, combine remaining ingredients with a whisk to make your sauce.

5. Stirring frequently, bring the sauce ingredients to a boil.

6. Pour the sauce over the meat in the slow cooker. Stir well. Heat the sauce on low for another 30 minutes.

7. Ladle the hot meat and sauce into sanitized jars.

8. Lid the jars and process them in a pressure canner for 70 minutes at 10 PSI. If you are using quart jars, process at the same pressure for 90 minutes.

Serving suggestion: The meat can be served on a bun or just piled on a plate and paired with Sweet and Sassy Coleslaw (page 100).

Mexi-Meat

For instant gratification of those fiesta cravings, preserve some ground meat that is already seasoned and ready to fill a tortilla. Going with the "use what you've got" principle, you can use ground beef, ground chicken, or ground whatever for these flavorful pints.

Reducing the amount of fat is not only better for your waistline, it's better for the preservation of your food. A high-fat item is more vulnerable to spoilage. After precooking the meat, carefully drain the fat before adding the seasoning. If you really want your product to be lean, you can also rinse the meat under running water, but I usually skip that step.

Makes approximately 6 (1-pint) jars

1 tablespoon olive oil

2 large onions, finely minced

6 cloves garlic, finely minced

5 pounds ground meat

2 cans tomato paste

¼ cup chili powder

⅛ cup ground cumin

1. Add olive oil to a large stockpot and lightly sauté the onion and garlic.

2. Add your ground meat to the pot, stirring well to combine it with the onion and garlic.

3. Pour in enough water to cover the meat and veggie mixture.

4. Bring the contents of the stockpot to a boil, then reduce heat until the mixture is simmering lightly. Cook for about 20 minutes, stirring occasionally.

5. Using a metal colander, drain your meat mixture carefully.

6. Return the meat and veggie mixture to the stockpot and stir well to combine the tomato paste and spices.

7. Immediately ladle the mixture into prepared pint jars, leaving ½ inch of headspace.

8. Process the jars in a pressure canner for 90 minutes at 10 PSI, adjusting for altitude.

SERVING SUGGESTION: Use this meat anywhere you'd use freshly cooked taco filling—on nachos, topping a taco salad, filling a tortilla…the list is endless!

Sloppy Joe Filling

Some things taste better than they look, and this filling is one of those things. It's absolutely delicious, but once it cools in the jars, there is some separation. Use whichever ground meat you have on hand.

Don't be deterred by the lengthy prep time, as very little of it is hands-on. You can also reserve some Sloppy Joe meat for dinner instead of canning the entire batch.

Makes approximately 7 (1-pint) jars

6 pounds prepped tomatoes

2 cups chopped onions

2 cups chopped sweet bell peppers

2 cloves garlic, minced

1½ cups brown sugar

2 tablespoons paprika

½ cup apple cider vinegar

5 pounds lean ground meat

salt and pepper, to taste

1. Using a food processor, puree the tomatoes, onions, bell peppers, and garlic in batches.

2. Pour the vegetable puree into your slow cooker and cook it on low for about 6 to 8 hours with the lid askew. The volume should be reduced by half.

3. Stir in the sugar, paprika, vinegar, and salt and pepper and continue to cook on low for 2 to 4 more hours or until the mixture has reached the desired consistency.

4. On a stovetop, lightly brown ground meat and drain in a metal colander. Rinse if you want to reduce the fat content further.

5. Stir the drained beef into the sauce.

6. Ladle the sauce into sanitized pint jars.

7. Wipe the lips of the jars, then place the lids on.

8. Process in a pressure canner for 90 minutes at 10 PSI.

SERVING SUGGESTIONS: Remember, you may notice a bit of grease separated in your jar of sauce and meat. This is not unusual. You can either drain it off before reheating or stir it in. Once you've reheated your sauce, serve it on a bun for a classic Sloppy Joe, or even on a pita. Add a side of coleslaw! (See the recipe for Sweet and Sassy Coleslaw on page 100.)

Skinless Boneless Chicken

Raw-packing skinless boneless chicken results in a tender poached chicken that is delicious when cut up into chicken salads or when shredded and seasoned to be used in enchiladas or other recipes. For the sake of versatility, this recipe contains only very mild seasoning.

Each quart jar will hold approximately three average-sized chicken breasts or six chicken thighs. The following recipe is per jar, so multiply the ingredients as needed.

Although it can be done safely, I don't recommend canning bone-in chicken. The bones dissolve into gelatinous muck that is neither pretty nor tasty.

Makes 1 quart jar

1 clove crushed garlic	½ teaspoon sea salt
3 skinless boneless chicken breasts, or 6 skinless boneless thighs	½ teaspoon black pepper
	water as, needed

1. Place one clove of garlic in the bottom of each sanitized quart jar.

2. Add raw chicken pieces to the jar, pushing them down to pack tightly.

3. Add salt and pepper, and then fill the jar with water, allowing 1 inch of headspace.

4. Carefully slide a rubber spatula utensil down the interior sides of the jars, removing air pockets. Do not skip this step, or your jars may not seal. Wipe the rims of the jars.

5. Lid the jars and process in a pressure canner for 90 minutes at 10 PSI, adjusting for altitude.

Carnitas

This is the most fantastic way to can pork, ever! Carnitas can be used as taco or burrito filling, or you can serve it with refried beans and rice. Or, you can try not to burn your mouth and eat it directly from the skillet. Shoulder roast or stewing beef will work just as well as pork for this recipe. Use either orange juice concentrate or lime juice.

Makes approximately 8 (1-quart) jars

15 pounds of pork	½ teaspoon chili powder
Per quart jar:	½ teaspoon dried oregano
1 clove garlic, minced	⅛ teaspoon salt
⅛ cup minced onion	1 bay leaf
½ teaspoon ground cumin	1 tablespoon lime juice

1. If necessary, cut pork into bite-sized pieces. Trim the visible fat off the roast.

2. Add pork to quart jars, allowing room for the additional ingredients.

3. Top each jar with the seasonings above in the order listed. Do not add any additional liquid.

4. Wipe the rims of the jars with a paper towel dipped in vinegar, then put the lids on.

5. Process in a pressure canner for 90 minutes at 11 PSI.

SERVING SUGGESTIONS: Carnitas meat should be reheated by draining it and frying it in a cast-iron skillet. You'll end up with lovely, delicious, crispy bits. When the meat is cooked, mix the sauce back in and stir well until it's heated through.

El Pollo Mexicano

In case you can't tell, we're big fans of Mexican food in this house. This is a way to preserve boneless chicken that is immediately ready to fill enchiladas, burritos, and tacos. You can use chicken thighs or breasts for this recipe, and for those of you that don't enjoy cilantro, you can substitute parsley. Lemon juice, lime juice, and white vinegar are all equally effective in this recipe and can be substituted if needed.

Makes approximately 7 (1-quart) jars

10 pounds boneless, skinless chicken

4 pounds peeled, diced tomatoes

4 pounds mixed bell peppers

¼ pound hot peppers (optional)

1 pound diced onion

½ cup lemon juice

8 cloves garlic, minced

3 tablespoons chili powder

1 tablespoons ground cumin

⅛ cup chopped fresh cilantro

salt, to taste

1. Cut up chicken into bite-sized pieces and fill jars two-thirds of the way.

2. In a large, non-reactive bowl, mix all of the other ingredients together.

3. Ladle the vegetable and spice mixture over the chicken.

4. Use a rubber spatula to remove air pockets.

5. Process the jars in a pressure canner at 11 PSI for 90 minutes, adjusting for altitude.

CHAPTER 11

Beans, Beans, Beans

Beans are a pantry staple for many preppers, but they sure do take a long time to cook! This is fine in normal circumstances, where you just need to plan ahead, soak them, and let them simmer for a few hours.

However, in a grid-down situation, this can be easier said than done. I've cooked them on my wood stove before and it took an entire day, and required constant stoking of the fire to keep the heat up enough. It takes far too much fuel to make a humble pot of beans.

For this reason, I always have some jars of home-canned beans on my shelves. There's a lot of room for variety when home canning your beans. You can use whatever beans you have on hand for this: navy beans, white kidney beans, black beans, pinto beans, or even a mix of a few different kinds. And finally, if you need to, feel free to leave out the meat. Some have religious restrictions or follow a vegetarian diet. Just skip the addition of the meat and carry on with the rest of the instructions.

When canning beans, they must be soaked ahead of time, and then the pressure canning process will do the rest of the work. If you don't soak them, they may not get thoroughly cooked. This doesn't mean they're unsafe. However, they will be crunchy and will need to be cooked for an extra hour or so instead of merely being heated up. When canning beans, they must be totally covered with liquid and there must be room for them to expand.

Some question the price efficiency of canning my own beans instead of buying pre-canned beans at the store. This is a valid point—they end up, with the price of the power to can them and the use of a jar lid, to be about the same price as the conventional store-bought canned beans. But if you are using organic beans and comparing the home-canned to store-bought organic beans, doing it yourself is far cheaper.

And there are other reasons I like to can beans at home…

- I know exactly what is in the beans I can myself. I am certain they contain no high-fructose corn syrup, no additives to maintain texture or appearance, and no hidden MSG.

- I'm assured of the quality of meat that I'm using. The pork in home-canned pork and beans will be the high-quality pork you have selected, hopefully from a local farm that does not use growth hormones or antibiotics, and where they don't feed their pigs GMO feed.

- Store-canned beans are often seasoned with some kind of sludgy meat by-product. You don't even want to think about it.

- I know the beans have been carefully washed and sorted by hand, not sifted through some machine that might not catch everything I would.

Yeah, I know, I'm picky! But once you taste these beans, you'll see why it's worth it to go the extra mile to make them.

Basic Pork and Beans

This recipe has worked on any type of bean I've tried it with, including pinto, navy, black, red kidney, white kidney, chickpeas (garbanzos), and black-eyed peas. Adjust the meat you add according to what will blend nicely with your bean of choice, as well as how you intend to use the beans in the future.

As I mentioned previously, I tried this once without pre-soaking the beans and the results were poor. The beans had to be further cooked in liquid when I opened the jar. This was resolved by two different methods: adding them to soup and letting them cook for another hour or two when I opened the jar, or making oven-baked beans.

Makes approximately 7 (1-quart) jars

5 pounds dried beans	6 small onions, cut in half
1 to 2 pounds ham, salt pork, or bacon	water or broth, as needed
salt (optional)	12 bay leaves

1. Rinse and sort dried beans, then soak them in hot water for at least 2 hours (but overnight is better).

2. Discard the soaking water, then bring to a boil in fresh water or broth.

3. Drain the beans again, this time reserving the cooking water.

4. Distribute the pork evenly across sanitized quart jars.

5. Top the meat with soaked beans, filling each jar no more than three-quarters full.

6. Add to each jar a pinch of salt, if using, 2 bay leaves, and an onion.

7. In the bean pot, bring 6 cups of the reserved liquid, or broth, to a boil. Add more liquid if necessary.

8. Ladle the hot liquid over the beans, leaving 1½ inches of headspace. The beans must be totally covered with liquid, and there must be room for them to expand.

9. Lid the jars and process in a pressure canner at 10 PSI for 75 minutes for pints or 90 minutes for quarts, adjusting for altitude.

Mexican Pork and Beans

At serving time, these beans can be heated as is, or mashed and lightly fried in a cast iron skillet for refried beans.

Makes approximately 7 (1-quart) jars

5 pounds dried black beans or pinto beans

1 to 2 pounds salt pork or bacon

water or broth, as needed

¼ teaspoon garlic powder

¼ teaspoon onion powder

⅛ teaspoon ground cumin

¼ teaspoon chili powder

1 tablespoon tomato paste

½ onion per jar

salt (optional)

1. Rinse and sort dried beans, then soak them in hot water for at least 2 hours.

2. Discard the soaking water, then bring to a boil in fresh water or broth.

3. Drain the beans again, this time reserving the cooking liquid.

4. Distribute the pork evenly across the jars.

5. Top the meat with soaked beans, filling each jar no more than three-quarters full.

6. Add to each jar a pinch of salt, garlic powder, onion powder, cumin, chili powder, tomato paste, and half an onion.

7. In the bean pot, bring 6 cups of the reserved liquid, or broth, to a boil. Add more liquid if necessary.

8. Ladle the hot liquid over the beans, leaving 1½ inches of headspace. The beans must be totally covered with liquid, and there must be room for them to expand.

9. Lid the jars and process in a pressure canner at 10 PSI for 75 minutes for pints or 90 minutes for quarts, adjusting for altitude.

BBQ Beans

These are your basic Southern picnic beans, delicious served warm, cold, or at room temperature. Use navy, kidney, white kidney, or pinto beans. Brown sugar can be substituted with muscovado sugar.

Makes approximately 7 (1-quart) jars

5 pounds dried beans

1 to 2 pounds salt pork, ham, or bacon

6 cups tomato juice

½ cup apple cider vinegar or white vinegar

1 tablespoon garlic powder

1 tablespoon onion powder

1 tablespoon chili powder

2 tablespoons dry mustard

1 teaspoon liquid smoke

salt (optional)

2 tablespoons brown sugar per jar

½ onion per jar

cooking liquid, as needed

1. Rinse and sort dried beans, then soak them in hot water for at least 2 hours.

2. Discard the soaking water, then bring beans to a boil in fresh water or broth.

3. Drain the beans again, this time reserving the cooking water.

4. Distribute the pork evenly across your jars.

5. Top the meat with soaked beans, filling each jar no more than three-quarters full.

6. Bring tomato juice, vinegar, spices, and liquid smoke to a boil.

7. Add to each jar a pinch of salt, if using, 2 tablespoons brown sugar, and half an onion.

8. Ladle the hot tomato juice over the beans, leaving 1½ inches of headspace. If necessary, add some of the cooking water. The beans must be totally covered with liquid and there must be room for them to expand.

9. Lid the jars and process in a pressure canner at 10 PSI for 75 minutes for pints or 90 minutes for quarts, adjusting for altitude.

Boston Baked Beans

These beans are tangy and delicious right out of the jar. The liquid is the classic Boston Baked Beans sauce, containing no tomato product. It thickens up beautifully during the canning process. We often add these beans to speed up a batch of homemade chili. The usual bean for this recipe is the navy bean, but I've also made it with pinto beans and the results were delicious.

Makes approximately 7 (1-quart) jars

5 pounds dried beans

1 pound bacon or salt pork

6 tablespoons dark molasses

2 tablespoons white vinegar

2 tablespoons onion powder

1 tablespoon salt

2 teaspoon dry mustard

½ teaspoon ground cloves

cooking liquid, as needed

1. Rinse and sort dried beans, then soak them in hot water for at least 2 hours.

2. Discard the soaking water, then bring beans to a boil in fresh water.

3. Drain the beans again, this time reserving the cooking water.

4. Distribute the pork evenly across your jars.

5. Top the bacon with soaked beans, filling each jar no more than three-quarters full.

6. In the bean pot, bring 6 cups of the reserved liquid to a boil. Stir in the rest of the ingredients, simmering until they are well combined.

7. Ladle the hot molasses mixture over the beans and pork, leaving 1 inch of headspace. If you didn't make enough molasses mixture so that there is more than 1 inch of headspace, add more liquid as necessary.

8. Lid the jars and process in a pressure canner at 10 PSI for 75 minutes for pints or 90 minutes for quarts, adjusting for altitude.

Hoppin' John

This classic black-eyed pea dish is a traditional New Year's Day meal in many parts of the world, said to bring the person who eats it on prosperity throughout the coming year.

Unlike the other recipes in this section, the black-eyed peas should *not* be soaked ahead of time.

Makes approximately 6 (1-quart) jars

2 pounds chopped salt pork, bacon, or ham

3 pounds dried black-eyed peas

6 cloves garlic, crushed

2 cups diced green bell pepper

2 cups prepped, diced fresh tomato

2 large onions, finely chopped

finely diced jalapeño pepper, to taste (optional)

hot water, as needed

1. Layer the ingredients in each of your jars in the order listed, leaving 1 inch of headspace.

2. Pour hot water over the contents of the jars, allowing 1 inch of headspace for the peas to expand.

3. Use a rubber utensil to slide around the edges of the jar to remove air pockets. Add more liquid if necessary.

4. Lid the jars and process in a pressure canner at 10 PSI for 90 minutes, adjusting for altitude.

PART 3

Dinner Is in the Jar

CHAPTER 12

Soups and Stews

What could be nicer on a cold winter day than a piping hot bowl of soup? Piping hot soup that came from a jar that you canned a couple of months previously! One of the best things about canning is that you can put dinner on the table in the time it takes to heat something to boiling. I will never forget the first time I popped open a home-canned jar of beef stew. Not only was it delicious, tasting like it had been simmered all day long, but it was an instant-gratification meal.

Canning entire meals is the perfect solution for preppers. Very little fuel will be required to heat a home-cooked meal, each jar is loaded with a variety of protein sources and veggies, and you know that you're getting high-quality ingredients instead of mystery by-products.

When making soup, I recommend layering the ingredients. I don't always precook the soup because the flavors will meld beautifully during the pressure canning process. And as I mentioned before, I'm kind of lazy, so why would I want to make extra work for myself?

The reason for layering is more than just laziness, though. It is so that you get a somewhat equal amount of each item in your soup. Otherwise, you run the risk of having a jar of really chunky, meaty soup and a jar that is mostly broth. The other benefit is that this is a quick and easy method for preparing lots of delicious, healthy meals!

Basically Better Tomato Basil Soup

One of our family favorites is tomato basil soup. For a little variation on the traditional, this soup is delightful with yellow or orange tomatoes. You can use any variety of tomatoes for this soup, but I like to use the juicier tomatoes since there is no need to cook them down for hours to get a thick consistency.

This is a simple, per-jar recipe since tomato harvests vary, and if your garden is anything like mine, they provide you with an ongoing but difficult-to-predict supply for several weeks.

Makes 1 quart jar

INGREDIENTS PER JAR

1½ pounds peeled tomatoes

¼ onion

1 clove garlic

1 teaspoon balsamic vinegar

1 teaspoon honey

canning salt, to taste

black pepper, to taste

1 tablespoon dried basil

1. In a blender, puree together all ingredients except for the basil, until it reaches the desired consistency. Some people like it to be very smooth, while others prefer a slightly chunkier soup.

2. Fill your jars with soup straight from the blender, then add your dried basil to the top.

3. Wipe the rim, then put the lid on the jar.

4. Process the soup in a pressure canner at 10 PSI for 20 minutes, adjusting for altitude.

SERVING SUGGESTIONS: If you like creamy tomato soup, heat the contents of your jar, then stir in ¼ cup of milk or cream, heating only long enough to warm it through. Grilled cheese sandwich is optional but delicious!

Bestern Southwestern Chicken Soup

This Mexican-inspired soup is a family favorite. Be sure to soak the beans ahead of time for best results. There is no need to pre-cook them, as they will cook nicely in the pressure canner as long as they have been soaked.

Makes approximately 7 (1-quart) jars

3 cans diced tomatoes, juice reserved

6 cups chicken broth

3 tablespoons chili powder

1 tablespoon cilantro

1 tablespoon ground cumin

3 cups chicken, cooked and shredded

3 cups black beans, rinsed, sorted, and pre-soaked

2 cups corn kernels

1 onion, finely diced

4 cloves garlic, minced

1 bell pepper, diced

salt and pepper

1. In a large stockpot, stir together tomatoes, broth, chili powder, cilantro, cumin, salt, and pepper. Bring this mixture to a boil.

2. Layer the other ingredients evenly in your jars.

3. Top the layered ingredients with your hot broth mixture, leaving 1 inch of headspace. If you run out of broth, it's fine to top up your jars with water, as the flavors will have plenty of time to blend.

4. Lid your jars and process in a pressure canner for 90 minutes at 11 PSI. Be sure to adjust for altitude.

SERVING SUGGESTIONS: Serve your delicious soup topped with a dollop of plain yogurt or sour cream and some crumbled tortilla chips. For heartier fare, you can serve this over brown rice or quinoa.

Splendiferous Split Pea Soup

On a crisp, cold winter day, what could be more deliciously comforting than some fresh crusty bread and a bowl of smoky split pea soup? This recipe is a household favorite and ideal for canning. When you heat it up, you may need to add some water or broth to get it to the consistency that you prefer. I heartily recommend the ham broth recipe on page 151! Otherwise, if you leave it as is, you might be able to eat it with a fork!

This soup can't be layered. You'll need to cook up a big pot of it for canning to get the right consistency.

Makes approximately 6 (1-quart) jars

½ pound ham or bacon, diced (about 1 cup)

1 tablespoon olive oil

2 whole onions, finely chopped

6 cloves garlic, finely minced

6 cups split peas, rinsed and sorted

15 quarts of water

3 carrots, peeled and cut into chunks

3 to 4 bay leaves

1 tablespoon dried thyme

1. In a big Dutch oven or stockpot, sauté ham or bacon in olive oil until it is lightly browned.

2. Add in onions and garlic and sauté for about 2 more minutes.

3. Stir in all of the rest of the ingredients and bring to a boil.

4. Reduce heat and simmer, covered, for an hour to an hour and a half, until all ingredients are soft.

5. Even if you prefer a puree, I recommend canning it at this point. It will cook more during processing and most likely be the consistency you desire. If not, you can puree it at the time you heat it up for dinner.

6. Fill quart jars and allow 1 inch of headspace.

7. Process in the pressure canner for 90 minutes at 12 PSI, adjusting for altitude.

SERVING SUGGESTIONS: Go crazy and sauté a little bacon or ham for the top of the soup. Drizzle with sour cream, and serve with fresh crusty bread for dipping.

Great Golumpki Soup

Isn't the word "Golumpki" simply fantastic? Golumpki is the Polish name for cabbage roll, a fantastic yet time-consuming Eastern European delicacy that I am way too lazy to make.

So I turned it into soup because soup is easy, particularly in this layered raw-pack recipe. You can substitute pork for beef in this recipe.

Makes approximately 6 (1-quart) jars

3 pounds ground beef

6 cups shredded cabbage

1½ cups shredded carrots

2 medium onions, finely chopped

6 cloves garlic, minced

12 cups tomato juice

3 tablespoons brown sugar

1½ cups white vinegar

2 tablespoons dried oregano

2 tablespoons dried basil

salt and pepper, to taste

1. Layer meat, cabbage, carrots, onion, and garlic in equal parts across your jars.

2. In a large stockpot, combine tomato juice, sugar, vinegar, salt, pepper, and herbs. Heat this mixture to a simmer for 10 minutes.

3. Top the ingredients in the jars with your canning liquid. If needed, add more water, leaving 1 inch of headroom.

4. Process in a pressure canner at 11 PSI for 90 minutes. Be sure to adjust for altitude.

SERVING SUGGESTIONS: This soup is great as is, right out of the jar. For a heartier meal, you can add 1 cup of cooked rice, or cook 1 cup of rice into the liquid to give it more of a casserole consistency. Some people like it topped with a drizzle of sour cream.

Autumn Garden Stew

One great way to make use of all those tasty root veggies in your fall garden is with a hearty stew. Based on what you have available, you can mix and match veggies to your heart's content. Do *not* add flour or any other thickener to your stew until you are ready to eat it. Thickeners do not store well when canned, and they turn your meal into a clumpy mess.

This is a raw-pack recipe, meaning the meat and vegetables will cook in the pressure canner and do not need to be cooked ahead of time.

Use whatever type of beast meat you have on hand. For root vegetables, I suggest potatoes, sweet potatoes, parsnips, turnips, and rutabaga. Feel free to mix and match these veggies, or just pick your favorite and go with that one.

Makes approximately 7 (1-quart) jars

8 cups water or stock

1 tablespoon dried thyme

½ tablespoon dried marjoram

2 tablespoons dried parsley

4 pounds cubed beast

4 to 6 cups cubed root vegetables

2 cups carrot rounds

3 cups finely chopped onion

6 cloves garlic, crushed and minced

1. In a stockpot, combine water or stock, thyme, marjoram, and parsley, and bring to a boil.

2. Meanwhile, layer meat and vegetables into your jars.

3. Pour the hot liquid over the layered meat and vegetables. Add more water if needed. Leave 1 to 1½-inches of headspace.

4. Lid your jars and process them in your pressure canner for 90 minutes at 10 PSI. Be sure to adjust for altitude.

SERVING SUGGESTIONS: When you are ready to serve your stew, add 1 tablespoon of flour to ½ cup water and whisk into a paste. Stir this into your stew as you heat it up to make a thick, hearty gravy.

Chicken-Needs-Noodles Soup

If your family craves homemade chicken noodle soup when they are under the weather, reach for this instead of the familiar red and white can. When you can your own soup, you know that you aren't feeding your family deadly neurotoxins in the form of MSG, which is present in nearly *all* conventional canned soups on the market.

This soup has everything but the noodles, and the reason for this is that noodles break down and turn into a goopy mess when they are canned. Some people will tell you that they have canned soup with noodles for years and that the noodles are perfect, but I have never had success. When it is soup time, simply pour it into a pot, bring it to a boil, and throw in the amount of pasta that you want.

You can make this with any kind of poultry.

Makes 1 quart jar

2 uncooked boneless skinless chicken thighs or 1 chicken breast

¼ teaspoon dried oregano

½ cup carrot rounds

¼ teaspoon dried basil

¼ cup chopped celery

¼ teaspoon dried thyme

¼ cup finely grated onion

⅛ teaspoon salt

2 cloves fresh garlic, mashed

water, as needed

1. Layer your ingredients in the jars.

2. Bring water to a simmer.

3. Ladle hot water into the jars until you have 1 inch of headspace remaining. You will look at this and notice that there is way more liquid than chicken and veggies, but that's important because you need additional liquid for serving time, when you cook the pasta.

4. Lid your jars and pressure can at 12 PSI for 90 minutes, adjusting for altitude.

Serving suggestion: If you're feeding someone with a tummy ailment, add a little bit of ginger to the soup when re-heating. You can also add some fresh minced garlic at serving time. Add whatever grain works for you at the moment: pasta, rice, orzo, quinoa, and barley are all delicious.

Mexican-Texican Cowboy Chili

Chili is the perfect meal for a snowy winter day. This recipe and the recipe on page 132 provide two very different takes on the traditional chili and are both enormously popular at our house. They are assembled using the layering method and are raw-packed, making it simple to create up to 7 family dinners at one cooking session—or even more, if your canner can hold it!

Another great thing about chili is the nutritional value: it's loaded with protein, vitamins, and fiber! The canned chili that you get from the grocery store generally contains lower quality meats, the least expensive vegetables available, and relies on artificial flavors and chemicals like MSG for its taste. If you want a heat-and-eat meal, home-canned chili makes a far better addition to your pantry.

This recipe is the classic thick, savory chili, loaded with meat and beans. Use whatever meat you have on hand. It's best seasoned with beer, but if you don't have any you can use water instead. Either crushed tomatoes or tomato juice can be used.

Makes approximately 6 (1-quart) jars

10 cups crushed tomatoes

1 can beer

½ cup chili powder

3 tablespoons ground cumin

1 tablespoon salt

1 tablespoon minced parsley

4 pounds ground meat

2 pounds dried pinto beans, pre-soaked

1 cup diced onion

4 cloves garlic, minced

1 cup diced bell pepper

diced jalapeño peppers, to taste (optional)

water, if needed

1. In a stockpot, bring crushed tomatoes, beer, chili powder, cumin, salt, and parsley to a boil.

2. Layer your meat, dried beans, onions, garlic, bell pepper, and jalapeño, if using, evenly across your jars.

3. Pour your hot liquid mixture over the layered ingredients, then top off with water, leaving 1 inch of headspace.

4. Process at 10 PSI for 90 minutes in your pressure canner. Be sure to adjust for altitude.

Tips for Perfect Home-Canned Chili

- Soak the beans ahead of time and they will cook perfectly during the canning process.

- Feel free to take liberties with the ingredients, using whatever you are able to source healthfully. The seasoning is the important part!

- Raw pack all of the ingredients and load the jars using the layering method.

- The chili will thicken as it sits on the shelf. You may need to thin it with a small amount of water or tomato juice at serving time.

Sweet and Spicy Chili

This recipe is awesome if you happen to acquire some venison or other game. A lot of people are uncomfortable with the unfamiliar "wild" flavor of the meat, and this extremely well-seasoned chili hides that. Minus the jalapeños, this produces a very kid-friendly flavor.

Ground meat works just as well as stew meat for this recipe. Molasses can be substituted for brown sugar.

Makes approximately 7 (1-quart) jars

8 cups tomato puree

½ cup apple cider vinegar

½ cup brown sugar

½ cup chili powder

1 tablespoon salt

1 teaspoon dry mustard

4 to 6 pounds cubed beast

3 cups dried red kidney beans, pre-soaked

1 slice bacon per jar

2 large onions, diced

6 cloves garlic, minced

1 cup diced bell pepper

finely minced jalapeño pepper, to taste

water, as needed

1. In a stockpot, bring tomato puree, apple cider vinegar, brown sugar, chili powder, salt, and dry mustard to a boil.

2. Layer your raw meat, dried beans, bacon, onions, garlic, and peppers evenly across your prepped jars.

3. Pour your hot liquid mixture over the layered ingredients, then top off with water as needed, leaving 1 inch of headspace.

4. Process at 10 PSI for 90 minutes in your pressure canner. Be sure to adjust for altitude.

SERVING SUGGESTIONS: When serving your chili, shred the bacon with a fork and stir it in.

Chicken Vegetable Chowder Starter

The reason I call this recipe a "starter" is because you'll be adding some dairy at serving time. The USDA strongly cautions against canning anything with dairy products or thickeners, but you can have the basis of this delicious chowder. You can also serve it simply as a chicken and vegetable soup if you don't have access to dairy products. This is a raw-pack, per-jar recipe.

Makes 1 quart jar

2 thighs or 1 breast boneless skinless chicken, cut into bite-sized pieces

½ cup corn

¼ cup green peas

¼ cup diced carrots

½ cup diced potatoes

⅛ cup diced celery

⅛ cup finely minced onion

⅛ cup diced red pepper

1 clove garlic, smashed

salt and pepper, to taste

½ teaspoon dried parsley

¼ teaspoon dried thyme

⅛ teaspoon dried dill weed

water, as needed

1. In clean quart jars, layer the ingredients in the order listed above.

2. Fill each jar with water, leaving ⅛ inch of headspace. Use a rubber spatula to remove any air pockets.

3. Process this in a pressure canner for 90 minutes at 11 PSI, adjusting for altitude.

1. At serving time, pour half of the liquid out of the jar. Reserve this for thickening your roux.

2. In a saucepan, melt 1 teaspoon of butter, then make a roux by whisking in 2 tablespoons of flour until combined well.

3. Add the liquid and whisk it together with the roux, dropping the heat to low.

4. Meanwhile, in another saucepan, heat the rest of the contents of your jar.

5. When everything is heated through, add ½ cup of milk or cream to your roux, whisking to combine.

6. Combine everything by stirring in the contents of your other saucepan. Serve immediately.

SERVING SUGGESTIONS: Garnish this with some crisp, crumbled bacon and sour cream.

MINESTRONE

Enjoy some garden goodness with this delicious vegetable soup. This recipe is vegetarian, but if you want to add meat to it, the canning process is the same.

If you drain your tomatoes in a colander before making sauce, you can use the broth that was drained from your tomatoes as the basis of this soup. The USDA recommends that when canning soup, no more than half the jar should be filled with solid ingredients, and the rest should be your broth or other liquid.

These ingredients are merely suggestions; use any assorted vegetables you have on hand or wish to have in your soup. This recipe is perfect for using up bits of garden odds and ends.

Makes 1 quart jar

SUGGESTED INGREDIENTS

corn

carrots

peas

green beans

fresh shelled beans

potatoes, diced

winter squash, cut into cubes

zucchini, diced

celery, chopped

SEASONINGS, PER JAR

1 tablespoon minced onion

1 clove garlic, minced

¼ teaspoon dried basil

¼ teaspoon dried oregano

¼ teaspoon dried thyme

½ bay leaf

salt and pepper, to taste

tomato juice or stock, as needed

1. Layer the solid ingredients evenly across your jars, making sure to keep them below the halfway full point.

2. Top each jar with the appropriate seasonings.

3. Ladle tomato juice or stock over your ingredients.

4. Wipe the rims of the jars, put on the lids, and process for 90 minutes at 11 PSI, adjusting for altitude.

CHAPTER 13

Main Dish Meals in Jars

These main dishes require only quick side dishes to allow you to have a great meal on the table faster than you can say "drive-thru." The simple addition of a grain like brown rice, quinoa, or pasta, and depending on availability and season, perhaps a vegetable or salad on the side, will make it seem like you slaved all afternoon over a hot stove as opposed to just opening a jar and boiling some water. (Don't worry. It'll be our little secret.)

A few of these meals, like the Stroganoff on page 138, would be enhanced by stirring in some sour cream at serving time. See the "Serving Suggestions" at the end of each recipe.

All ingredients are uncooked unless the recipe specifically states otherwise. This protects vegetables from getting mushy and overcooked, and allows the meat to get pressure-cooked, which creates a flavorful broth and provides a fork-tender result.

Hungarian Goulash

Goulash is generally served over spaetzle, egg noodles, rice, or mashed potatoes. This is best with *real* Hungarian paprika; without it, you won't get an authentic flavor.

Makes approximately 7 (1-quart) jars

4 tablespoons Hungarian paprika

2 teaspoons dry mustard

1 tablespoon olive oil

4 onions, quartered

4 cloves garlic, minced

4 pounds stewing meat

4 carrots, sliced into large pieces

2 bell peppers, diced

6 potatoes, diced

6 cups water, plus more as needed

½ cup red wine vinegar

1 (6-ounce) can tomato paste

salt and pepper, to taste

1. In a bowl, mix Hungarian paprika, dry mustard, salt, and pepper.

2. In a large stockpot, heat olive oil and begin to sauté your onions and garlic.

3. Dip your stewing meat in the spice mixture, then place the meat in the stockpot to brown with the garlic and onions. You only need to brown lightly—the meat doesn't need to be cooked.

4. In quart jars, layer your meat and vegetable mixture, carrots, peppers, and potatoes.

5. Add 6 cups of water, vinegar, and tomato paste to the stockpot and mix with any drippings or spices that remain after browning the meat. Bring this mixture to a boil.

6. Ladle hot liquid into jars over the layered contents. Use a table knife or spatula to remove any air pockets in the jars. If necessary, add more water, allowing 1 inch of headspace.

7. Lid the jars and process in your pressure canner for 1 hour and 15 minutes at 10 PSI, adjusting for altitude.

SERVING SUGGESTIONS: When heating your goulash, whisk in 1 tablespoon of flour to thicken the sauce. Once it is hot, stir in ½ cup of sour cream or plain yogurt, and heat only until the sour cream is warmed through.

Beef Stroganoff

Beef stroganoff is delicious served over egg noodles or rice. Use stewing beef or sliced sirloin for best results.

Makes approximately 7 (1-quart) jars

4 to 5 pounds beef, chopped or sliced

2 onions, finely chopped

4 cloves garlic, finely chopped

4 cups sliced mushrooms

1 tablespoon butter

2 tablespoons Worcestershire sauce

water, as needed

salt and pepper, to taste

1. In a large stockpot, sauté beef, onions, garlic, and mushrooms in butter until lightly browned.

2. Stir in Worcestershire sauce, salt, pepper, and enough water to deglaze the stockpot. Use a metal utensil to scrape the bottom of the pot to loosen the flavorful pieces there.

3. Add 2 cups of water and stir well, bringing to a boil.

4. Ladle the stroganoff into sanitized quart jars, distributing the cooking liquid evenly across the jars. Don't worry about adding more liquid—when the meat cooks, it will add flavorful juices.

5. Process in your pressure canner for 90 minutes at 10 PSI, adjusting for altitude.

SERVING SUGGESTIONS: When you are ready to serve the beef stroganoff, heat the sauce then stir in 1 cup of sour cream or plain yogurt. Continue heating the sauce at a low temperature only until the addition is warmed through.

Cajun Jambalaya

The beautiful thing about jambalaya (aside from its incredible blend of Cajun flavors) is that it's one of those use-what-you've-got kinds of recipes: ham, chicken, sausage, or even all three. At serving time, you can toss in some fresh shrimp, too.

This recipe won't look like the other "meal" recipes; it will look more like a soup. You need to cook rice in the flavorful broth at serving time. Use quart jars, and make sure each one contains at least 2 cups of liquid to cook the rice.

Andouille sausage is the traditional sausage choice for this dish, but any smoked sausage will work. Use green or red pepper bell, or a combination of both. Tabasco is a good option for the hot pepper sauce, but you can use your favorite.

Makes approximately 7 (1-quart) jars

1 tablespoon olive oil

3 to 4 pounds boneless, skinless chicken thighs and breasts, cut into bite-sized pieces

2 cups smoked sausage, cut into chunks

2 cups chopped onion

2 cups chopped bell pepper

2 ribs celery, chopped

6 cloves garlic, minced

2 tablespoons smoked paprika

2 tablespoons dried thyme

cayenne pepper, to taste

2 tablespoons Cajun spice blend

6 cups peeled tomatoes with juice, divided

¼ teaspoon hot pepper sauce

4 cups chicken broth

4 cups water

salt and pepper, to taste

1. In a large stockpot, warm the olive oil and lightly brown the first 6 ingredients.

2. In a small bowl, mix paprika, salt, pepper, thyme, cayenne, and Cajun spice blend.

3. Sprinkle the vegetable and meat mixture with spice mixture, then add tomatoes and hot sauce, and stir well to combine.

4. Ladle the ingredients into sanitized quart jars, filling them no more than halfway.

5. Meanwhile, place the broth, tomato juice, and water in the stockpot and bring it to a boil, deglazing the bottom of the pot.

6. Ladle 2 cups of hot liquid into each jar, allowing 1 inch of headspace. You can top up with water if you need to.

7. Lid the jars and process in a pressure canner for 90 minutes at 10 PSI, adjusting for altitude.

SERVING SUGGESTIONS: When it's jambalaya time, add 1 cup of rice to the contents of your jar. Bring it to a boil, reduce heat, put the lid on, and simmer until your rice is cooked and most or all of the liquid has been absorbed. Remove from heat and fluff rice. Allow the dish to sit for 5 minutes covered, then enjoy the rich Cajun flavor!

Chicken Cacciatore

The rich herbed tomato sauce and the tender chicken will not last long on the pantry shelves, because as soon as you serve one jar of it, your family will beg you to make it again!

To make life simple, this is a raw-pack recipe. A mix of chicken breasts and thighs provides a good flavor, but you can choose just one or the other if you'd like.

Makes approximately 7 (1-quart) jars

4 pounds boneless, skinless chicken breasts and thighs, cut into bite-sized pieces

2 cups red and green bell peppers, cut into chunks

3 medium onions, cut into eighths

2 cups sliced mushrooms

8 cloves garlic, smashed

1 bottle red wine

4 cups diced tomatoes with juice, divided

2 tablespoons dried oregano

2 tablespoons dried basil

2 tablespoons dried thyme

salt and pepper, to taste

1. Layer chicken, peppers, onions, mushrooms, and garlic in quart jars. Season with salt and pepper.

2. In a large stockpot, bring wine, tomatoes, and herbs to a boil. Season with salt and pepper.

3. Ladle hot liquid over the layered ingredients in your jars.

4. Lid the jars and process them in your pressure canner for 90 minutes at 11 PSI, adjusting for altitude.

SERVING SUGGESTIONS: When heating the cacciatore, stir in a small can of tomato paste to thicken the sauce. Serve over pasta or rice, with a side of garlic bread.

Marinara Sauce and Meatballs

Meatballs go through the canning process very nicely. I have always made them eggless because my youngest daughter was allergic to eggs when she was little. It seems as though these slightly dry meatballs hold together better during the canning process than the ones that contain egg. You can use whatever type of ground meat you have on hand.

I usually freeze bread to make breadcrumbs; to actually make the crumbs, I use a food processor. Always account for the amount of salt in your breadcrumbs and adjust the salt in your recipe accordingly.

Makes approximately 7 (1-quart) jars

5 pounds ground meat

2 cups very fine crumbs

2 tablespoons salt

2 tablespoons dried parsley

1 tablespoon garlic powder

1 tablespoon onion powder

½ batch Snowfall Spaghetti Sauce (page 103)

1. Combine the meat, breadcrumbs, salt, parsley flakes, garlic powder, and onion powder in a large bowl, using your hands to mix well.

2. Form very firm meatballs. They should fit nicely in the palm of your hand.

3. Place 8 to 10 meatballs into each sanitized quart jar. Don't overfill the jars with meatballs, because you want to leave room for sauce.

4. Heat marinara sauce until it is simmering, about 10 minutes.

5. Cover the meatballs with hot marinara sauce.

6. Very gently use a rubber spatula to remove air pockets so that the sauce completely fills the jar, allowing 1 inch of headspace at the top.

7. Process for 90 minutes in a pressure canner at 10 PSI, adjusting for altitude.

Meat Sauce Marinara

Use any type of ground meat for this recipe. For a lower-fat recipe, you can rinse the meat after browning on the skillet. If you choose to do this, add the seasonings after you rinse it instead of during the cooking process.

Makes approximately 7 (1-quart) jars

3 to 4 pounds ground meat

1 tablespoon onion powder

salt and pepper, to taste

½ batch Snowfall Spaghetti Sauce (page 103)

1. Brown the ground meat in a large skillet over medium heat, stirring in seasonings.

2. Drain the meat and blot it with a paper towel to remove some of the fat.

3. Fill quart jars halfway with meat, then ladle hot spaghetti sauce over the meat. Use a rubber spatula to remove air pockets and add more sauce, if needed.

4. Wipe the lip of the jar carefully, and put the lids on.

5. Process the meat sauce in your pressure canner for 90 minutes at 10 PSI, adjusting for altitude.

Marinara with Sausage and Peppers

The flavor of the sausage gives a whole new spin to your basic (yet incredibly delicious) marinara sauce. This goes nicely with a chunkier pasta like rigatoni or fusilli.

Makes approximately 7 (1-quart) jars

6 pounds lean Italian sausages

3 tablespoons olive oil

3 cups of red bell peppers, cut into long spears

2 large onions, diced

3 cups halved button mushrooms

½ cup brown sugar

½ batch Snowfall Spaghetti Sauce (page 103)

1. Slice Italian sausages into chunks.

2. Heat olive oil in a large skillet over medium heat. Sauté Italian sausage until it is lightly browned.

3. Remove sausage and add peppers, onions, and mushrooms. Sauté veggies until caramelized.

4. Layer sausage and veggies evenly across your quart jars.

5. Add brown sugar to marinara. Mix well.

6. Add marinara sauce to jars, leaving ½ inch of headspace.

7. Wipe the lips of the jars carefully, and put the lids on.

8. Process the meat sauce in your pressure canner for 90 minutes at 10 PSI, adjusting for altitude.

Pot Roast Dinner

This is basically like canning roast beast, except it is a complete meal. Each jar will provide a hearty dinner for two. Use whatever type of meat you have on hand.

Makes 1 quart jar

1 pound roast

1 clove garlic

1 small cooking onion, quartered

1 large carrot, cut into chunks

1 potato, cut into bite-sized pieces

salt and pepper, to taste

water, as needed

1. Place a hunk of roast in each quart jar, leaving enough space to layer the additional ingredients.

2. Add potatoes, carrots, garlic, onions, salt, and pepper to each jar.

3. Pour water into the jars over the meat and veggies. Using a rubber spatula, run it down the sides of the jars to remove any air pockets, then add more water if needed. Allow 1 inch of headspace.

4. Use a cloth with some vinegar on it to wipe the lips of the jars.

5. Lid the jars.

6. Using your pressure canner, process the jars for 90 minutes at 10 PSI, adjusting for altitude.

SERVING SUGGESTIONS: When you are ready to serve your roast, use the canning liquid to make gravy.

Apple-Spiced Pork Chops

For the flavor of pork chops and applesauce, try this tasty meal in a jar. Wide-mouth jars work best in this recipe.

You can thicken the liquid from the jar to make an apple-flavored gravy, and you can serve this with rice, quinoa, or mashed potatoes. Thick-sliced lean roast works just as well as pork chops in this recipe.

Makes approximately 6 (1-quart) jars

3 small cooking onions, cut into quarters

6 cloves garlic

1 tablespoon brown sugar per jar

⅛ teaspoon ground cloves per jar

6 pounds boneless pork chops

3 to 4 tart apples, cut into eighths

salt and pepper, to taste

1. In each jar, layer half a cooking onion, a clove of crushed garlic, sugar, ground cloves, salt, and pepper.

2. Trim the visible excess fat off your pork and cut it into pieces that will easily fit in the jars.

3. Fill the each jar halfway with pork, then layer 4 slices of apple in each.

4. Add more pork, then top off the jars with the rest of the apples. Do not add any cooking liquid.

5. Wipe the rims of the jars with a vinegar-dampened cloth, then cap the jars.

6. Pressure can at 11 PSI for 90 minutes, adjusting for altitude.

Sweet and Sour Chicken

Enjoy some Asian flair with this recipe that is sure to become a family favorite. At serving time, you can thicken the canning liquid and serve this dish over rice and noodles with some steamed veggies on the side.

Optionally, you can use pork for this recipe. Red or yellow bell peppers are best for this recipe, but you can use whichever you like best. If no whole pineapples are available near you, you can substitute three cans of pineapple chunks and reserve the juice. Coconut aminos can be substituted for soy sauce.

Makes approximately 7 (1-quart) jars

3 cups pineapple juice

¾ cup brown sugar

1¼ cups apple cider vinegar

6 tablespoons soy sauce

4 tablespoons tomato paste

1 teaspoon ground ginger

4 cloves garlic, minced

5 pounds boneless skinless chicken, cut into bite-sized pieces

2 medium onions, diced

3 bell peppers, diced

1 whole pineapple, cleaned and diced

crushed chili pepper, to taste (optional)

1. In a large saucepan, bring to a boil pineapple juice, sugar, vinegar, soy sauce, tomato paste, ginger, and garlic, stirring frequently. Simmer until the sugar is dissolved and the mixture is smooth.

2. In your jars, layer chicken, onions, peppers, and pineapple. If you're using crushed chilis, add them now.

3. Ladle the sauce over the contents of the jars.

4. Wipe the rims of the jars, put the lids on, and process in a pressure canner at 11 PSI for 90 minutes, adjusting for altitude.

Irish Brisket and Potatoes

This jar makes a hearty meal with the versatility to be used for either breakfast or dinner. Be very, very careful to use a light hand with the spices and if your brisket is already spiced, leave them out altogether, especially the pickling spice. You will also want to omit adding any extra salt in this recipe.

Makes approximately 7 (1-quart) jars

6 pounds corned beef brisket

10 cups water

2 tablespoons pickling spice (optional)

5 cups diced potato

2 cups carrots, cut into chunks

2 onions, diced

1. Trim your brisket to remove as much fat as possible, then cut it into bite-sized pieces.

2. Put water and pickling spice, if using, into a stockpot and bring it to a boil.

3. Layer potatoes, carrots, and onion in the bottom third of your wide-mouth quart jars.

4. Layer brisket on top of the potatoes and allow 1 inch of headspace.

5. Ladle spiced water into the jars, maintaining the inch of headspace. I strain the spices out, because they greatly intensify while this sits on the shelf.

6. Using a rubber spatula, remove any air pockets.

7. Wipe the rims of the jars with a paper towel dipped in vinegar, then put the lids on.

8. Process in a pressure canner at 11 PSI for 90 minutes, adjusting for altitude.

SERVING SUGGESTIONS: You can serve this with boiled cabbage for a classic Irish dinner. You can also drain the liquid and dump the contents of the jar onto a cutting board. Dice the meat, potatoes, and carrots, then fry it up in a hot cast-iron skillet for a tasty corned beef hash. Top it with a fried egg for a hearty breakfast.

Beef Burgundy

This is a family favorite that can be served over mashed potatoes or egg noodles. Even better, you can thicken the sauce and, for extra French flair, serve over a toasted sourdough baguette. Any red meat roast will go well with this recipe.

Makes approximately 7 (1-quart) jars

6 slices bacon, diced

3 pounds halved mushrooms

6 cloves garlic, minced

6 onions, quartered

2 bottles red wine

1 tablespoon dried thyme

4 cups of carrots, cut in large chunks

6 pounds roast beef, cut into bite-sized pieces

salt and pepper, to taste

1. In a large stockpot, lightly brown the bacon. Then, reserve the fat and lightly sauté mushrooms, garlic, and onion.

2. Drain bacon and sautéed veggies on a plate lined with a paper towel.

3. Add red wine, salt, pepper, and thyme to the stockpot and bring it to a boil. Reduce heat and allow it to simmer.

4. Divide your sautéed vegetables, bacon, and the carrots across your wide-mouth quart jars. Top with your roast.

5. Ladle the red wine mixture into the jars, maintaining 1 inch of headspace.

6. Wipe the rims of the jars, then put the lids on.

7. Process in a pressure canner for 90 minutes at 10 PSI, adjusting for altitude.

CHAPTER 14

Making the Most of Leftovers

Picture it: It's the day after a holiday, and your refrigerator is stuffed to the point that you have to lean against the door to close it and you never want to see another bite of turkey, ham, or roast beef again.

So what can a thrifty person do with all of that delicious bounty? Preserve it!

Of course, preserving leftovers isn't only limited to Thanksgiving, Christmas, and Easter, although holiday feasts are known for the boon that they can give to your pantry. If you have some jars and fresh lids, your kitchen already contains everything you need to add an abundant amount of food to your stockpile.

All sorts of leftover goodies can be put back for future use, adding to your shelves full of home-preserved ingredients. Don't let anything go to waste. Many people wait too long to preserve the food and end up having to throw most of it in the trash.

Meat, veggies, soup, and even cranberry sauce will all make beautiful additions to your home-canned stock. Use these recipes as a guideline to adapt your leftovers into nutritious, homemade meals in jars.

Make it a tradition to spend a day in the kitchen once the holidays are over, and put away that food for later! Keep in mind the rules that you've learned for preserving your own food, and you can safely stash away all sorts of stuff!

Note that some of these recipes will not include yields because the quantities will vary based on the ingredients you use.

Roast Beast Leftovers

This is a great way to preserve virtually any roast that you have in abundance—beef, bison, venison, or pork, for example. Use any spices that you'd like for these leftovers, but be certain to use a light hand with spices, as they will intensify during canning.

Also remember not to add flour to the broth for "gravy" because it doesn't store well. Instead, make fresh gravy from the broth when you open the jar.

cooked roast	onion, quartered
1 clove garlic per jar, crushed	broth, red wine, or water to top off each jar

1. When your leftover roast is cool, take the section you intend to preserve and slice it thinly.

2. In the bottom of each jar, place your clove of crushed garlic and a wedge of onion, as well as any spices you intend to use.

3. Place the slices of beast vertically into the jars, packing the jar loosely.

4. Top the meat with the liquid of your choice. Allow 1 inch of headspace.

5. Process the meat for 90 minutes in a pressure canner at 10 PSI, adjusting for altitude.

Home-Canned Ham How-To

In a totally different stratosphere from Spam, cans of flaked ham, and the big, pear-shaped cans of ham sitting in mysterious congealed substances, you'll find home-canned ham.

Every Christmas I get a spiral-cut, naturally cured ham. It is pricy, but very delicious. I bake it in a nice orange-brown sugar glaze and we pick away at it for a few days. We always reserve our cooking liquid in the refrigerator to use when we're canning.

Then, in order to get our money's worth, I spend several hours canning the abundant leftovers.

It's important to note that home canned ham gets *incredibly salty* as it sits in the jar. It doesn't work well as a stand-alone meat, but it's a delicious addition to casseroles, beans, soups, or scalloped potatoes. Because of this, I prefer to can ham in pint jars instead of quart jars.

As mentioned, the flavor of the ham becomes much more intense as it sits in the jar. Be careful about adding salt when you open the jar, and be sure to add the ham to another food you are preparing. But you can do a lot with canned ham:

- The ham pieces can be sautéed and added to scrambled eggs or in place of bacon to top baked potatoes or soup.

- The ham and broth can be used to make red-eye gravy.

- The ham pieces can be used in casseroles and scalloped potatoes.

- The broth is a delicious base for soups, cooking rice or wheat berries, or cooking beans or other legumes.

Home-Canned Ham

This is the simplest, most basic way to can your leftover ham.

1. Begin with your rather motley looking piece of ham on the bone.

2. Using a sharp knife, remove as much ham as possible from the bone.

3. Meanwhile, bring your reserved cooking liquid to a boil on the stove. You may want to add 2 cups of water to thin it down to a broth-like consistency.

4. Place the pieces into pint jars. (You will have some fattier pieces that you won't want to eat—put those aside for the broth you're going to make in the recipe that follows.)

5. Fill pint jars with ham pieces.

6. Ladle the hot broth in, leaving 1 inch of headspace. If you don't have broth, you can use water or chicken broth for this.

7. Wipe the lip of the jar with a cloth dipped in vinegar and lid the jars. At 10 PSI, pressure can pints for 75 minutes, adjusting for altitude.

Ham Broth

Don't stop at simply canning the meat—now it's time to make broth. This broth can be used as a soup base, for cooking grains like rice, or in any recipe requiring liquid in which the smoky flavor of ham would be tasty. I like to use my slow cooker to make broth, but this can also be simmered all day long on the stovetop. Don't add salt, or the broth will be far too strong.

ham bone and leftover meat	bay leaf
2 onions, quartered	2 carrots, peeled
2 to 6 cloves garlic, smashed	enough water to fill the slow cooker

DIRECTIONS FOR BROTH

1. Place the ham bone and any unappetizing pieces of meat into your slow cooker.

2. Add onion, garlic, carrots, and bay leaf.

3. Cover the contents of the slow cooker with water and fill to the top.

4. Place the lid on and then cook on low for 10 hours.

5. Use a metal colander to strain the broth.

6. Use broth immediately or see canning directions, below.

DIRECTIONS FOR CANNING

1. Ladle the hot strained broth into quart jars, leaving 1 inch of headspace.

2. Wipe the lip of the jar with a cloth dipped in vinegar and lid the jars.

3. Pressure can for 90 minutes at 10 PSI, adjusting for altitude.

Sugar Baked Ham

This recipe is per jar and is a great way to put away those endless leftovers after a big dinner! I use pint jars for canning ham, as mentioned previously. This sweeter ham is a yummy addition to baked beans or any other dish that is sweet and savory.

Makes 1 pint jar

1 teaspoon prepared grainy mustard

3 tablespoons brown sugar

1 teaspoon apple cider vinegar

4 (½-inch thick) slices ham

4 whole cloves

1. Make a paste of the mustard, sugar, and vinegar, and spread it on one side of the ham.

2. Roll each slice and insert them into the jar.

3. Top each ham roll with a clove. Do not add liquid.

4. Clean off the lip of the jar and cap them with lids and rings.

5. Process the ham in a pressure canner for 75 minutes at 10 PSI, adjusting for altitude.

Shredded Poultry

If you have lots of turkey or chicken leftovers after a meal, you can shred the meat with two forks and then jar it up for use in recipes like enchiladas, soft tacos, or casseroles, or you can drench it in barbecue sauce for sandwiches.

Makes 1 quart jar

1 clove garlic, crushed

¼ onion

roasted poultry, shredded

¼ teaspoon sea salt

black pepper, to taste

water, as needed

1. Place garlic and onion in the bottom of jars.

2. Fill the jars with shredded poultry, topping off with salt and pepper.

3. Pour hot water over the contents of the jars.

4. Carefully slide a table knife or rubber spatula down the inside of the jars, removing air pockets. Leave 1 to 1½-inches of headspace.

5. Lid the jars and process in a pressure canner at 13 PSI, 90 minutes for quarts or 75 minutes for pints, adjusting for altitude.

Turkey or Chicken Stock

After you remove the meat from the carcass to can it, you'll be left with a rather desolate-looking carcass. Don't be deterred by the ugliness of this naked bird! This is canning *gold*! Be sure to scavenge through your refrigerator for vegetables that can be added to the cooking pot. These deeply golden, rich, meaty jars are an excellent base for turkey or chicken and dumplings, as well as any type of soup.

I always give our dog a big treat after making this stock: a bowl of turkey with gristle, fat, and skin. She's a little on the skinny side because she runs constantly when she's outside, so I think that the occasional fat intake is good for her. She also likes the mushy carrots. I usually divide the "sludge" into a few different servings of treats for her.

An important note about spices: Sage tastes horrible when canned. If it is normally an ingredient in your chicken soup, add it when you heat and serve it. It's really, really, really bad when canned, and even my dog wouldn't taste the broth I had canned with sage in it. And she eats dirty shoes!

Makes approximately 8 (1-quart) jars

carcass, giblets, neck, and other lower quality cuts of meat

assorted uncooked vegetable

1 head garlic

2 to 4 onions

2 tablespoons salt

spices of choice

DIRECTIONS FOR STOCK

1. Place all ingredients in the slow cooker.

2. Fill the slow cooker right to the top with water.

3. Put the slow cooker on low for 12 to 14 hours and let it simmer undisturbed overnight.

4. The next day, strain the contents of the slow cooker into a large container. I use a big soup pot and a metal colander.

5. Allow the bones to cool, and then remove any meat that you would like to add to your soup.

DIRECTIONS FOR CANNING

1. If you have chicken or turkey you'd like to add, cut it into bite-sized pieces. I like a mixture of light meat and dark meat for this purpose. Also cut up the meat you removed from the slow cooker.

2. Place approximately 1 cup of turkey in each of your quart jars.

3. Add 1 to 2 cloves of garlic to the jars.

4. You will have a rich, dark, beautiful stock from the overnight slow cooker project. Ladle this over your cut-up turkey and garlic, leaving 1 inch of headspace at the top of the jars. Add water as needed.

5. Wipe the lip of your jars with a cloth dipped in white vinegar.

6. Place the lids on and process them in your pressure canner for 90 minutes at 10 PSI, adjusting for altitude.

Canning Cranberry Sauce

If you have leftover cranberry sauce, you may can it for future use. I like to use teeny little half-pint jam jars for this.

1. Heat the cranberry sauce to a simmer on the stovetop.

2. Ladle the sauce into sanitized jars, leaving ¼ inch of headspace.

3. Wipe the rims of the jars, then place the lid on them.

4. Process in a water bath canner for 15 minutes, adjusting for altitude.

Soup à la Leftovers

The ultimate leftover canning concoction has to be the eclectic "Leftover Soup." An example of a soup I made one year contained carrots that were cooked in honey, green beans with some butter, some diced sweet potatoes, corn with butter, and roasted chicken. So for this recipe, round up whatever veggies that you have left over. Don't worry if they have some butter and seasonings on them—it will all add to the rich flavor of your soup. Raid your veggie drawer, chop your crudités into bite-sized pieces, and add them raw to your jars, because they'll cook beautifully during the canning process.

fresh or leftover vegetables, in any combination

diced potatoes (optional)

1 cup diced meat per jar

1 clove garlic per jar

2 tablespoons chopped onion, per jar

1 cup Turkey or Chicken Stock (page 153) per jar

water, as needed

1. Place your vegetables and potatoes, if using, into a large bowl and combine well.

2. Add 1 cup of your vegetable mixture to each sanitized quart jar.

3. Add 1 cup of meat/poultry to each jar, adding garlic and onion on top.

4. Top your veggies and meat with 1 cup of the delicious stock you made earlier.

5. Fill the jar the rest of the way with water. The flavors will blend—don't worry!

6. Wipe the lip of your jars with a cloth dipped in white vinegar and then place the lids on.

7. Process the soup in your pressure canner for 90 minutes at 10 PSI, adjusting for altitude.

Serving Suggestion: If you want a different type of soup, add 2 tablespoons of tomato paste to each jar and season with some Italian spices, like basil and oregano. At serving time, add some cooked rice, barley, or pasta to your soup to make a heartier meal.

CHAPTER 15

Creative Canning

In this section, we're going to launch out into the wide world of canning, Granny-style. Yes, we'll still stick to the modern rules of safety, but sometimes the things we wish to preserve don't show up in the canning books.

HOW TO SAFELY CAN YOUR OWN RECIPES

Canning recipes are great to have, but they aren't necessary. Some experts might disagree, but I firmly believe that if you have a grasp on food safety principals and canning basics, you can preserve your own recipes.

However, you do need to follow the basics rules of canning. When canning your own recipes, search for instructions on how to can the separate ingredients. Determine the processing time of your own recipes by using the time for the ingredient that requires the *longest* processing time. For example, say you're canning a roast with carrots, onions, and beef. The carrots require 20 minutes, the onions require 30 minutes, and the beef requires 90 minutes. Thus, 90 minutes of pressure canning is required to safely can this recipe.

You should also note whether the individual ingredients have special requirements for when they are being canned. Always use the longest time and the most stringent requirements to make sure your food is safe.

The *USDA Complete Guide to Home Canning*[16] has a lot of great information on safely canning many different separate ingredients. And it's a free download!

I have to stress that the onus for your family's safety is upon you. Because I cannot predict every single ingredient of every single recipe a person might wish to can, I can't give you a comprehensive list of dos and don'ts.

If there is any doubt as to the safety of something you intend to can, don't risk it. I believe that you possess the good judgment and ability to look up your separate ingredients and omit them if they should not be canned. It's not worth risking the health of your family.

In no particular order, here are some DIY tips for canning your own recipes:

- If your recipe calls for grains, like pasta or rice, omit them during the canning process and add them at serving time.

- If your recipe calls for the addition of flour or dairy as a thickener, omit those ingredients during the canning process. It is far tastier (and safer) to add those ingredients during the reheating process. When I make beef stew, for example, I can the stew ingredients and herbs in a broth or water, then when reheating, I dip out a small ladleful of liquid and stir in flour to make a hearty gravy.

- Some ingredients have flavors that "turn" when you can them. Sage, for example, tastes terrible when canned. I have also learned from unpleasant experience that spinach gives a terrible flavor to the entire dish when canned.

- Keep in mind that the spices and seasonings you use will intensify as the jar sits there in your cupboard. For some foods, like spaghetti sauce, this is a great bonus! For others, it can be overwhelming.

---

16   http://nchfp.uga.edu/publications/publications_usda.html

- If you heat something up, like a soup or stew, and find the flavor is overpowering, often you can rectify the situation by adding a few cups of broth or water. Ham, in particular, develops incredibly strong flavors, so I only use canned ham as an ingredient in other dishes, rather than as a meal by itself. It works well in a pot of beans or in scalloped potatoes.

- Just because it looks unpleasant in the jar doesn't necessarily mean that it's bad. Meat often looks rather unappetizing in the jar because the fat separates and floats to the top or the sides of the jar. Simply stir the fat back in or dispose of it.

- It can be risky to can foods that are extremely high in fat, because they become rancid far more easily than leaner meats. Strain out some of the fat before canning to avoid unnecessary risk.

Once you have the hang of canning using pre-made recipes, it's really simple to modify these and create your own recipes.

HAPPY CANNING!

Whether you're getting ready for a simple power outage due to a storm, the possibility of a financial downturn, or an apocalyptic scenario, there's more to it than just going to the store and stacking the shelves of your pantry with those goods. You need skills.

A crisis is not a time for trial and error. When you first begin canning, you'll have a few failures. Maybe your jars won't seal properly, maybe your family will hate the recipe, or maybe you'll discover that your canner gasket isn't in good shape, making it impossible to get up to the right pressure.

This is not a big deal when your back-up supply is around the corner and open 24 hours a day, 365 days a year. It's a much bigger deal when you are preserving a limited supply of food to get your family through the winter. Get your trial and error out of the way now, and make delicious goodies at the same time. Win-win.

Our lives are so dependent on everything humming along like it normally does that when there is a change in our situation, it can be paralyzing.

Suddenly, we're been transported from the modern world of conveniences to a time when everything was a lot more work. To thrive during those episodes, you need the right set of skills. We have the benefit of being able to combine modern food safety science with Granny's recipes, and it gives us the best of both eras.

I wish you a season with a bountiful harvest and successful, happy canning!

Helpful Hints

FRUIT CANNING QUICK REFERENCE	
FRUIT	TIME AT SEA LEVEL
Apple slices	25 minutes
Apricots	35 minutes
Berries	25 minutes
Cherries	30 minutes
Figs	55 minutes Add 2 tablespoons lemon juice
Grapefruit	15 minutes
Grapes	25 minutes
Nectarines	35 minutes
Oranges	15 minutes
Peaches	35 minutes
Pears	30 minutes
Pineapple	25 minutes
Plums	30 minutes

These fruit-canning times are all based on the raw-pack method of canning fruit in quart jars.

If you are canning a combination of fruits, look up the times for each ingredient individually. Always go with the longest time to make certain that your food is canned safely.

VEGETABLE CANNING QUICK REFERENCE

FOOD	TIME FOR PINTS AT SEA LEVEL	TIME FOR QUARTS AT SEA LEVEL
Asparagus	30	40
Beans (green or yellow)	20	25
Beets	30	35
Carrots	25	30
Corn	55	85
Lima Beans	40	50
Okra	25	40
Peas (field)	40	40
Peppers	35	not recommended
Potatoes (white)	35	40
Potatoes (sweet)	65	90
Pumpkin	55	90
Squash (winter)	55	90

Remember, vegetables are a low-acid food and must be processed in a pressure canner with a baseline of 11 PSI, and adjustments for altitude.

BASIC JAM-MAKING GUIDELINES

FRUIT	SPECIAL INSTRUCTIONS	PROCESSING TIME
Apricot	Peel, slice in half to pit	5 minutes
Blackberry	optional step: mill to remove seeds	10 minutes
Blueberry	optional step: puree	7 minutes
Cherry	Pit with a cherry pitter, chop before cooking	10 minutes
Grape	Mill to remove seeds	10 minutes
Huckleberry	Check for stems	10 minutes
Peach	Peel, slice in half to remove pits	10 minutes
Plum	Slice in half to remove pits	5 minutes
Raspberry	Crush with a potato masher	10 minutes
Strawberry	Remove cores, mash with a potato masher	10 minutes

ALTITUDE ADJUSTMENTS

ELEVATION	TEMPERATURE AT WHICH WATER BOILS
0 (Sea Level)	212°F
2,000	208°F
4,000	204°F
6,000	201°F
8,000	197°F
10,000	194°F

ADJUSTMENTS FOR WATER BATH CANNING

ELEVATION	ADDITIONAL TIME
1,000–2,999	+5 minutes
3,000–5,999	+10 minutes
6,000–7,999	+15 minutes
8,000–10,000	+20 minutes

ADJUSTMENTS FOR PRESSURE CANNING

ELEVATION	ADDITIONAL PRESSURE
1,001–2,000	+ 1
2,001–4,000	+ 3
4,001–6,000	+5
6,001–8,000	+5
8,000–10,000	+5

VOLUME CONVERSIONS

U.S.	U.S. EQUIVALENT	METRIC
1 tablespoon (3 teaspoons)	½ fluid ounce	15 milliliters
¼ cup	2 fluid ounces	60 milliliters
⅓ cup	3 fluid ounces	90 milliliters
½ cup	4 fluid ounces	120 milliliters
⅔ cup	5 fluid ounces	150 milliliters
¾ cup	6 fluid ounces	180 milliliters
1 cup	8 fluid ounces	240 milliliters
2 cups	16 fluid ounces	480 milliliters

WEIGHT CONVERSIONS

U.S.	METRIC
½ ounce	15 grams
1 ounce	30 grams
2 ounces	60 grams
¼ pound	115 grams
⅓ pound	150 grams
½ pound	225 grams
¾ pound	350 grams
1 pound	450 grams

TEMPERATURE CONVERSIONS

FAHRENHEIT (°F)	CELSIUS (°C)
135°F	57°C
194°F	90°C
212°F	100°C
225°F	107°C
240°F	115°C

Index

Acknowledgments

First of all, thank you to my girls, who have suffered through many failed taste experiments and games of "Is This Recipe a Crapper or a Keeper?" I'm so proud of your accomplishments and of the wonderful human beings you have both become. I love you with all my heart, and everything I do, I do for you.

Thank you to my blogger buddies for your support and friendship over the years. I love it that I can bounce ideas off you, discuss the work-related quirks unique to our occupations, and just hang out with others who completely get it: Gaye, Lizzie, Tess, both Lisas, Melissa, Laurie, Scott, Mac, Jim, and Cat.

And thank you so much, the folks who read my books, visit my websites, and take my classes. Thank you for the years you've read what I have written, contributed to the conversations on my websites, and supported me by sharing the articles that I write. I wouldn't be living my dream of being a writer without you being readers.

About the Author

Daisy Luther is a coffee-swigging, gun-toting, homeschooling blogger. She writes about current events, preparedness, food, frugality, and the pursuit of liberty on her websites, The Organic Prepper and DaisyLuther.com She is the cofounder of Preppers University, where she teaches intensive preparedness courses in a live online classroom setting.

Daisy is also the author of *The Pantry Primer: A Prepper's Guide to Whole Food on a Half Price Budget*, *The Prepper's Water Survival Guide: Harvest, Treat, and Store Your Most Vital Resource*, and *Have Yourself a Thrifty Little Christmas and a Debt-Free New Year*.